APPLE TV 4K|HD
Complete User Guide

A Comprehensive Illustrated, Practical Guide with Tips & Tricks to Mastering The Apple TV 4K|HD and tvOS 13

Raphael Stone

Contents

Chapter 3 Siri and Dictation

Chapter 4 Maximizing your Apple TV

Chapter 5 Music

Chapter 6 Photos

Chapter 7 The App Store

Chapter 8 Podcast

Chapter 9 iTunes movies and TV shows

Chapter 12 Restart, Reset, Update

Chapter 13 Accessibility

Chapter 14 Safety and Handling

Introduction

If you're an Apple TV 4K/HD owner, the new version of tvOS, appropriately called tvOS 13, has just landed – bringing Apple Arcade, multi-user support, and a fresh home screen to Apple TV.

The Apple TV 4K can handle all 4K resolution content, with HDR10 and Dolby Vision supported, so the main new standards are covered – and (depending on the TV you've connected it to) the pictures look fantastic. From the flyover screensavers to the menu interface, everything packs in more pixels and looks sharper for it.

Apple TV 4K is also the only video streaming device to support both Dolby Atmos and Dolby Vision formats. The announcement came during Apple's WWDC 2018 keynote and came alongside the news that iTunes will now stock Dolby Atmos-enabled films and TV shows.

Since tvOS (the operating system that both the Apple TV 4K and standard Apple TV use) first appeared. it's really improved. Universal search is getting better all the time, and if you subscribe to Apple Music it makes the Apple TV a competent jukebox as well as a top-tier movie streamer.

The speedy A10X processor means you should be able to navigate the interface and load apps a hair faster than before, and Dolby Vision is a real asset to the streaming device as it's a format that few streaming devices support right now. We bring to you a complete user guide to master your Apple TV 4K/HD and the new tvOS 13 features, tips and tricks.

Chapter 1

Set up and get started

Set up Apple TV

To use Apple TV, you need:

- A high-definition or 4K TV with HDMI

- An HDMI cable to connect Apple TV to your TV (for 4K HDR, you may require a compatible Ultra High Speed HDMI cable, sold separately)

- Access to an 802.11 wireless network (wireless streaming requires 802.11a, g, n, or ac) or an Ethernet network and broadband Internet

- An Apple ID for purchasing and renting, downloading apps from the App Store, and using Home Sharing

To take full advantage of Apple TV 4K's audio and visual capabilities, you'll need a TV that supports 4K, HDR, and Dolby Vision, and a sound system that is Dolby Atmos-compatible.

Set up Apple TV

Before you start, make sure you know your wireless network name (and password if the network is password-protected). If you're using a wired network, use an Ethernet cable to connect your Apple TV.

1. Connect one end of an HDMI cable to the HDMI port on your Apple TV, then connect the other end to the HDMI port on your TV.

2. Connect one end of the power cord to the power port on your Apple TV and the other end to a power outlet.

3. Turn on your TV, then select the HDMI input that's connected to your Apple TV.

   On some televisions, this may occur automatically.

4. Follow the onscreen instructions to set your Internet connection, single sign-on, and other setup items.

Set up Apple TV automatically with an iOS or iPadOS device

Alternatively, you can transfer your Wi-Fi network and password and Apple ID account information automatically to Apple TV from an iOS device with iOS 9.1 or later, or from an iPadOS device with iPadOS 13 or later.

1. When the Apple TV setup screen appears, unlock your iOS or iPadOS device and make sure Bluetooth® and Wi-Fi are turned on.

2. Touch your device to Apple TV and follow the onscreen instructions on your iOS or iPadOS device and Apple TV.

Note: Automatic setup doesn't transfer account information for third-party apps such as Netflix or Hulu, and doesn't turn on iTunes Match or Home Sharing.

Set up your Apple ID on Apple TV

Your Apple ID is the account you use for just about everything you do on Apple TV, including buying movies or TV shows and subscribing to Apple TV channels in the Apple TV app , and downloading apps from the App Store . You can also use iCloud, which connects you and all of your Apple devices to share photos and more.

If you already have an Apple ID, enter it when you first set up Apple TV. If you don't already have an Apple ID, you can create one on the <u>Apple ID webpage</u>. You need only one Apple ID to use Apple TV app, iTunes, iCloud, and Game Center services.

Here are a few of the things you can do with your Apple ID on Apple TV:

- *Apple TV app:* Purchase or rent movies, buy TV episodes and seasons, and subscribe to Apple TV channels within the app. You can also access your purchases made with the same Apple ID on other devices.

- *Music:* If you're an Apple Music member, you can access millions of songs on Apple TV. With an iTunes Match subscription, all your music—including music you've imported from CDs or purchased somewhere other than the iTunes Store—can also be stored in iCloud and played on demand.

- *Apps:* Purchase   apps directly   on Apple   TV and download previous App Store purchases to Apple TV for free, anytime.

- *Game Center:* Play your favorite games with friends who have an Apple TV, an iOS or iPadOS device, or a Mac (OS X 10.8 or later).

- *Photos:* View your photos and videos from iCloud Photos, My Photo Stream, and Shared Albums.

- *Family Sharing:* Share purchased movies, TV shows, apps, and subscriptions on your Apple TV with up to six family members.

- *One Home screen:* Keep your installed apps and Home screen appearance the same across every Apple TV you own.

- *Sign in with Apple:* Sign in to apps with the Apple ID you already have, without filling out forms or creating new passwords. Apple doesn't track your activity and you're in control of your data.

- *AirPods support:* Listen with AirPods—no setup required. AirPods linked to your Apple ID connect automatically to your Apple TV.

Note: Not all features are available in all countries or regions.

Set password requirements for purchases

You can set whether or not Apple TV requires your Apple ID password to complete an iTunes Store or App Store purchase.

1. Open Settings on Apple TV.

2. Go to Users and Accounts > [*account name*] > Purchases, then select Always, After 15 Minutes, or Never.

Allow free downloads

You can set whether Apple TV requires your Apple ID password to allow free downloads in the iTunes Store or App Store.

1. Open Settings on Apple TV.

2. Go to Users and Accounts > [*account name*] > Free Downloads, then select Yes or No.

Set up single sign-on on Apple TV

Single sign-on simplifies access to entertainment apps like HBO GO and FXNOW. With it, you sign in only once on your Apple TV to get immediate access to all the supported apps that require your cable or satellite pay TV credentials.

Note: Some cable and internet providers support zero sign-on, which simplifies the sign-on process even further by automatically signing you in. Follow onscreen prompts during initial set up.

You can activate single sign-on during Apple TV setup, or in Settings. Once you've signed in, any other supported app you have access to will automatically authenticate you, eliminating the need to sign in again.

Tip: If you've saved passwords on your iOS device with iOS 12 or later, or on your iPadOS device with iPadOS 13 or later, you can autofill account passwords on Apple TV. See Set up accounts for other content providers on Apple TV.

Activate or deactivate single sign-on

1. Open Settings on Apple TV.

2. Go to Users and Accounts > TV Provider and select your TV provider.

3. Sign in with your user name and password for that provider.

   To deactivate single sign-on after you've signed in, select Sign Out.

Note: If you have more than one Apple TV, you must sign in once for each Apple TV to use this feature. Single sign-on is also available in iOS and iPadOS.

Manage subscriptions on Apple TV

You can modify or cancel subscriptions available on Apple TV, including Apple Music, Apple TV channels, Apple Arcade, or individual apps.

Manage your subscriptions

1. Open Settings on Apple TV.

2. Go to Users and Accounts > [*account name*] Subscriptions and select a subscription.

3. Follow the onscreen instructions to change or cancel your subscription.

Note: Not all features are available in all countries or regions.

Chapter 2

Understanding the Basics

Navigate Apple TV

The Home screen on Apple TV provides easy access to apps and settings. Navigate to any of the apps in the top row to see previews of available movies and TV shows, music videos, games, photos, and more.

You can also customize the top row with the apps you use the most.

Currently highlighted app

Use the Touch surface and buttons on the Siri Remote to navigate to, select, and open apps and content on Apple TV.

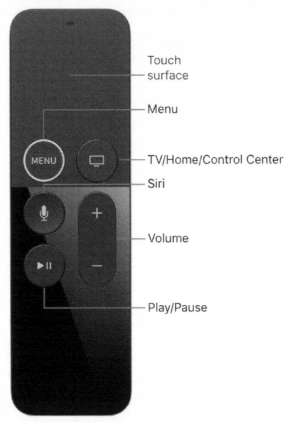

Touch
surface

Menu

TV/Home/Control Center

Siri

Volume

Play/Pause

Navigate apps, content, and lists

On the Siri Remote, do any of the following:

- *Navigate apps and content:* Swipe left, right, up, or down on the Touch surface.

  Onscreen, a highlighted app or content item expands slightly.

As you swipe the Touch surface area,
the highlighted app appears larger.

- *Preview content from the top row:* When you select an app in the top row, a preview of its content (movies, TV shows, or music videos, for example) begins playing in the background (if the app supports content previews). Swipe up on the Touch surface to play the current preview in full screen with audio and to access additional controls for playing the full video, getting more info, or browsing additional videos.

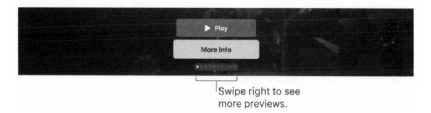

Swipe right to see
more previews.

- *Navigate lists:* Swipe up or down a few times on the Touch surface to scroll quickly. If there's an index next to the list, swipe right, then highlight a letter to jump ahead.

Select an item

13

- On the Siri Remote, swipe on the Touch surface to highlight the item, then press the Touch surface.

View additional menu options

- On the Siri Remote, press and hold the Touch surface.

  If you've highlighted an item that has additional options, they appear in a pop-up menu.

Return to the previous screen

- On the Siri Remote, press the MENU button.

Return to the Home screen

- *Return to the Home screen:* On the Siri Remote, press and hold the MENU button.

- *Return to the Apple TV app:* On the Siri Remote, press the Home button ⬒ to go to Up Next in the Apple TV app, or press twice to go to the Home screen.

  To change the Home button behavior,

Open Control Center

- On the Siri Remote, press and hold the Home button ⌨.

View open apps

- On the Siri Remote, press the Home button ▭ twice quickly.

Activate Siri

- On the Siri Remote, press and hold the Siri button 🎤.

You can navigate Apple TV with Control Center on an iOS device with iOS 11 or later, or on an iPadOS device with iPadOS 13 or later. You can also use the Apple TV Remote app (available from the App Store on your iOS or iPadOS device) to navigate, enter text, and control playback on Apple TV.

Enter text on Apple TV

There are several ways to enter text on Apple TV.

Use the onscreen keyboard

When a keyboard appears onscreen on Apple TV, use the Siri Remote to do any of the following:

- *Enter a character:* Swipe across the Touch surface—or tap the left or right side of the Touch

15

surface—to highlight an onscreen character, then press the Touch surface to select the character.

- *Change keyboards:* Press the Play/Pause button ▶❙❙, or swipe down and select uppercase, lowercase, numbers, or special symbols.

- *Enter an alternate character (such as a letter with an accent mark):* Highlight the character, then press and hold the Touch surface to select an option.

Use an iOS or iPadOS keyboard to type on Apple TV

Optionally, you can use your iOS or iPadOS device's keyboard to enter text on Apple TV.

Whenever a text field appears on Apple TV, a notification appears on your iPhone or iPad.

- On iPhone or iPad, tap the notification and enter text in the keyboard that appears.

   Text you enter on the iOS or iPadOS device automatically appears in the text field on Apple TV.

Use the Siri Remote

Whenever you see a text entry field, you can use your voice instead of using the onscreen keyboard.

- On the Siri Remote, press and hold the Siri button 🎤and say the text you want to enter. You can even speak individual characters—for example, when entering user names and passwords.

Manage your apps on Apple TV

Apple TV comes preloaded with a collection of apps on the Home screen. You can add other apps using the App Store🅰.

Open an app

- Using the Siri Remote, navigate to an app on the Apple TV Home Screen, then press the Touch surface to open it.

  Press and hold the MENUbutton to return to the Home Screen.

Note: You can switch between apps you've previously opened.

Change an app's settings

Some apps have a Settings menu within the app. For other apps, do the following:

1. Open Settings  on Apple TV.

2. Select Apps, select the app you want, then make changes.

Control what's playing on Apple TV

Whether you're watching a TV show or a movie, you're in control.

Play or pause

- On the Siri Remote, press the Touch surface or press the Play/Pause button ▶ ‖.

  When you pause playback, the playback timeline appears, showing elapsed and remaining time. The solid bar indicates how much of the item is cached (temporarily downloaded on Apple TV).

  Playhead ⌐   Caching progress ⌐

  0:03   -2:19

Rewind or fast-forward

You can move rapidly forward or backward through video in several ways. During playback, use the Siri Remote to do any of the following:

18

- *Preview video on the playback timeline:* Press the Play/Pause button ▶❙❙or press the Touch surface to pause playback, then swipe left or right on the Touch surface to move back or forward in time. A small preview window shows the current scene. Press the Touch surface again to start playback at the new position, or press the MENU button to cancel and resume playback at the original position.

- *Skip backward or forward 10 seconds:* Press the left or right side of the Touch surface to skip backward or forward. Press again to skip another 10 seconds.

- *Rewind or fast-forward continuously:* Press and hold the left or right side of the Touch surface to rewind or fast forward. Release to resume playback.

Get more info

- On the Siri Remote, swipe down on the Touch surface to show the Info pane. Swipe left or right to switch between panes.

19

Swipe to change panes.

Turn on subtitles and closed captioning (if available)

- On the Siri Remote, swipe down on the Touch surface to show the Info pane, swipe right to show the Subtitles pane, then swipe down and choose the option you prefer.

Select to turn on closed captioning.

Adjust Apple TV audio

You can control your TV or audio/video receiver volume with the Siri Remote. Additional audio controls let you change Airplay speakers, choose Bluetooth®

headphones, change the language audio track on a TV show or movie, or reduce loud sounds.

Adjust the volume

- Press the ✛or ━button on the Siri Remote.

Access audio controls

1. During playback, swipe down on the Touch surface of the Siri Remote to show the Info pane, then swipe to the Audio pane.

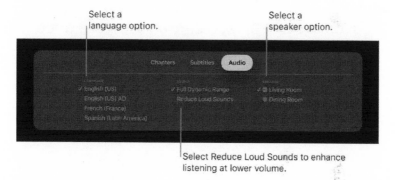

Select a language option.

Select a speaker option.

Select Reduce Loud Sounds to enhance listening at lower volume.

2. Do any of the following:

   ○ *Change the language:* Select a different audio language.

   ○ *Reduce loud sounds:* Select Reduce Loud Sounds to enhance dialogue and reduce loud sounds so as not to disturb others.

o *Change speakers:* Select another Airplay speaker on your network, or select connected Air Pods, Bluetooth speakers, or Bluetooth headphones.

Customize the Apple TV Home screen

You can change the order of apps on the Home screen and place your favorite apps in the top row. When you highlight an app in the top row, you get shortcuts that can take you to content without opening the app first.

On the Home screen, you can also delete apps from the App Store that you no longer use and change the appearance of backgrounds and menus between light and dark.

Rearrange apps

1. Using the Touch surface on the Siri Remote, highlight an app, then press and hold until the app starts to jiggle.

2. Swipe to move the app to a new location on the Home screen.

   Tip: Move your favorite apps to the top row of the Home screen. When you highlight a top-row app, shortcuts appear at the top of the screen.

3. Press the Touch surface again to save the new arrangement.

Create a folder   for apps

You can organize related apps into folders. For instance, you might store all of your music apps in a Music folder.

1. Using the Touch surface on the Siri Remote, highlight an app, then press and hold until the app starts to jiggle.

2. Drag the app over another app until a folder appears, then release.

3. Press the Touch surface again to save the new arrangement.

4. To change the name of the new folder, swipe up, then use the onscreen keyboard or dictation to enter a custom name.

5. Press the MENUbutton once to the close the onscreen keyboard, then press the MENUbutton again to return to the Home screen.

App folder

To delete a folder, drag all of its apps back to rows on the Home screen.

Move an app into a folder

1. Using the Touch surface on the Siri Remote, highlight an app, then press and hold until the app starts to jiggle.

2. Swipe to move the app over a folder, then release.

3. Press the Touch surface again to save the new arrangement.

4. Press the MENU button to return to the Home screen.

Delete an app

1. Use the Touch surface on the Siri Remote to select the app you want to delete, then press and hold until the app starts to jiggle.

2. Press the Play/Pause button ▶‖for more options, then choose Delete.

Deleting an app also deletes its data. You can download any app again that you've purchased on the App Store, free of charge, but the data may not be restored.

Change the appearance of Apple TV

1. Open Settings on Apple TV.

2. Go to General > Appearance, then select Light, Dark, or Automatic.

When set to Automatic, the appearance shifts from Light during daytime hours to Dark during nighttime hours.

Keep apps and the Home screen up to date across multiple Apple TVs

If you have more than one Apple TV associated with the same iCloud account, you can keep the same appearance and apps for each device. This makes it seamless to switch between an Apple TV in the bedroom and one in the living room, for example.

1. Open Settings 🔘 on Apple TV.

2. Go to Users and Accounts > iCloud and turn on One Home Screen.

Switch quickly between Apple TV apps

You can quickly switch between different apps on Apple TV without having to return to the Home screen. App-switching view on Apple TV works very much like the multitasking feature on iPhone or iPad.

See recent apps

- On the Siri Remote, press the Home button 🖵 twice quickly.

    Windows representing each of the open apps appear in a row on the screen.

Select a different app

- In app-switching view, swipe left or right on the Touch surface of the Siri Remote to navigate to a different app, then press the Touch surface to open the highlighted app (the app in the center of the screen).

Force the highlighted app to quit

- Swipe up on the Touch surface of the Siri Remote to force the highlighted app (the app in the center of the screen) to quit.

Leave app-switching view

- To leave app-switching view without changing apps, press the MENUbutton on the Siri Remote.

Use tvOS Control Center

Control Center gives you quick access to settings and controls for switching users, playing music, putting

Apple TV to sleep, and more. You can quickly switch between users in Control Center so that each person gets their own unique Up Next video list, video and music collections, and recommendations.

Open Control Center

- On the Siri Remote, press and hold the Home button⌐.

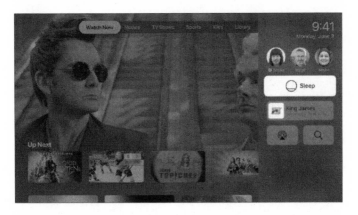

Switch to another user

1. In Control Center, swipe on the Touch surface of the Siri Remote to highlight a user, then press the Touch surface to select that user.

2. Sign in to the account.

   When you switch to another user, the previous user is signed out, and the TV and Music apps refresh with   the new users unique Up Next lists, video or music collections and recommendations.

Note: Switching   users does not change the Photos app or other settings associated with an iCloud account.

Access the current song in Music

When a song is playing   or paused in the Music app 🎵 on Apple TV, it's shown in Control Center.

- In Control Center, use   the Touch surface of the Siri Remote to select the currently playing song.

  The Music app opens to   the Now Playing screen.

Choose Airplay speakers

- In Control Center, use the   Touch surface of the Siri Remote to select the Airplay button 📶, then choose one or more   speakers.

Quickly access the Search app

- In Control   Center, use the Touch surface of the Siri Remote to select the Search button 🔍.

Put Apple TV to sleep

- In Control Center, use the touch surface of the Siri Remote to select Sleep.

Close Control Center

- Press the MENU button on the Siri Remote.

Connect the Siri Remote to Apple TV

The Siri Remote comes automatically paired with your Apple TV. If it disconnects or you get a replacement remote, you'll need to manually pair it to Apple TV.

You can pair the Siri Remote with only one Apple TV at a time. When you pair a remote, any other paired remote is automatically unpaired.

Pair the Siri Remote with Apple TV

1. Turn on Apple TV and position the Siri Remote so it's within 3 to 4 inches (8 to 10 cm) and pointing at the front of Apple TV.

2. Press and hold the MENU button and the Volume Up button +for 2 seconds.

   When the Siri Remote is successfully paired, an onscreen message appears.

Charge the Siri Remote

The Siri Remote has a rechargeable battery inside. With typical usage, you'll need to charge it a few times a year. An alert appears on the TV screen when the remote battery is running low; in Settings, you can go to Remotes and Devices > Remote to check the battery level. You can continue to use the Siri Remote while it's charging.

Lightning connector

Charge the Siri Remote

1. Connect one end of a Lightning cable to the Lightning port on the bottom of the Siri Remote.

2. Connect the other end of the cable to a computer USB port or to an Apple USB power adapter (sold separately).

The Siri Remote takes about three hours to fully charge.

Use the Siri Remote for game play on Apple TV

The Siri Remote included with Apple TV 4K and Apple TV HD (Late 2017) has an accelerometer, gyroscope, and built-in compass for playing a variety of games. Depending on the game, you can hold and move the remote in three dimensions (pitch, roll, and yaw). Some games respond to movements you make in the air with the remote.

Use the Remote Loop

- Attach the Remote Loop (sold separately) and maintain a secure grip on the Siri Remote to prevent injury or accidental damage to the Siri Remote or other property.

  To enhance game play, some apps may also work with a third-party Bluetooth® game controller or other accessory, or may require the use of a third-party Bluetooth game controller.

Game controller requirements are provided in the app's product page on the App Store.

Control the Touch surface sensitivity on Apple TV

You can customize the Touch surface on the Siri Remote to match your particular control style.

Change Touch surface tracking

1. Open Settings on Apple TV.

2. Go to Remotes and Devices > Touch Surface Tracking.

   Set Tracking to Fast to make smaller thumb movements move farther on the Apple TV screen. Set Tracking to Slow to reduce tracking sensitivity.

Control Apple TV with iOS or iPadOS Control Center

You can use Apple TV controls in Control Center on an iOS or iPadOS device. If you have an iOS device with iOS 12 or later, or an iPadOS device with iPadOS 13 or later, these controls are automatically activated when the device connects with Apple TV, such as during setup or when entering text with the keyboard.

You can control Apple TV using the Touch area and buttons.

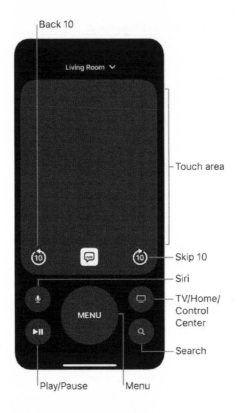

Note: Additional controls appear during playback. Tap the Skip Back button ↺⑩ to skip backward 10 seconds, or tap the Skip Forward button ⑩↻ to skip forward 10 seconds.

Open Apple TV controls in iOS or iPad OS Control Center

- On your iOS or iPadOS device, swipe to open Control Center, then tap the remote icon▓.

Add Apple TV controls to iOS Control Center manually

If you have a device with iOS 11 or later, you can activate Apple TV controls in Settings on the device.

1. On the iOS or iPadOS device, go to Settings > Control Center, then tap Customize Controls.

2. Tap the Add button ⊕ next to Apple TV Remote in the More Controls list to add it to Control Center.

Navigate and select apps, content, and lists

On the Apple TV Remote on your iOS or iPadOS device, do any of the following:

- *Navigate apps and content:* Swipe left, right, up, or down in the Touch area.

  Onscreen, a highlighted app or content item expands slightly.

As you swipe the Touch area, the highlighted app appears larger.

- *Navigate lists:* Swipe up or down a few times in the Touch area to scroll quickly. If there's an index next to the list, swipe right, then highlight a letter to jump ahead.

- *Select an item:* Swipe to highlight the item, then tap in the Touch area.

View additional menu options

- With an item highlighted on the Apple TV screen, touch and hold the Touch area in the Apple TV Remote.

  If you've highlighted an item that has additional options, they appear in a pop-up menu.

Use the app keyboard

When the onscreen keyboard appears on Apple TV, an iOS or iPadOS keyboard becomes available in the Apple TV Remote.

- Enter text in the iOS or iPadOS keyboard.

  Onscreen text updates as you type.

Adjust the volume

- Press the volume buttons on your iOS or iPadOS device.

Note: This works only with supported audio/video receivers.

Return to the previous screen or Home screen

On the Apple TV Remote on your iOS or iPadOS device, do any of the following:

- *Return to the previous screen:* Tap the MENU button.

- *Return to the Home screen:* Touch and hold the MENUbutton.

- *Return to the Apple TV app:* Tap the Home button ⌷once to go to Up Next in the Apple TV App.

View open apps

- On the Apple TV Remote on your iOS or iPadOS device, tap the Home button ⌷twice.

Open tvOS Control Center

- On the Apple TV Remote on your iOS or iPadOS device, touch and hold the Home button ⌷.

Activate Siri

- On the Apple TV Remote on your iOS or iPadOS device, touch and hold the Siri button🎤.

Connect the Apple TV Remote app

You can also control Apple TV using the Apple TV Remote app, which you can download from the App Store on an iOS or iPadOS device. The controls are similar to those found in iOS or iPadOS Control Center, with additional options (see the tasks below).

Set up the Apple TV Remote app

To use the Apple TV Remote app, you must connect it to your Apple TV.

1. Open the Apple TV Remote app on your iOS or iPadOS device, then select your Apple TV when it appears on the screen.

2. When a four-digit code appears on your Apple TV, enter the code on your iOS or iPadOS device.

Set up the Apple TV Remote app on an iOS device running iOS 11 or earlier

1. Download the Apple TV Remote app from the App Store on your iOS device.

2. Make sure your Apple TV and iOS device are connected to the same Wi-Fi network.

3. Open the Apple TV Remote app on your iOS device, then select your Apple TV when it appears on the screen.

4. When a four-digit code appears on your Apple TV, enter the code on your iOS device.

Use the app keyboard

When the onscreen keyboard appears on Apple TV, an iOS or iPadOS keyboard becomes available in the Apple TV Remote app.

- Enter text in the iOS or iPadOS keyboard.

    Onscreen text updates as you type. If the keyboard doesn't appear, tap the keyboard button⌨.

Show the Now Playing screen

The Now Playing screen in the Apple TV Remote app displays a still image of the current video along with basic playback controls.

- During video playback, tap Details, and then use the built-in controls in the Apple TV Remote app to control playback. Drag down from the top of the Now Playing screen to return to the Touch area.

Switch to   game mode

1. While playing a game using the Apple TV Remote app, tap   the Game button 🎮to switch to game mode.

2. Hold your iOS or iPadOS device in landscape orientation and use the Touch area and buttons to play the   game.

Stream content using Airplay with Apple TV

You can use Airplay to:

- Play videos or audio from your iOS or iPadOS device on Apple TV

- Play music, podcasts, and radio stations on multiple Airplay 2–enabled devices (such as Home   Pod   or   other speakers)   in   rooms throughout your house

- View the screen   of your Mac, iOS device, or iPadOS device on Apple TV

To stream content from a Mac, iOS device, or iPadOS device to Apple TV, both Apple TV and the shared device may need to be connected to the same Wi-Fi network.

Set up Apple TV to stream audio to Airplay 2– enabled devices

To stream audio from Apple TV to other audio devices such as Home Pod or other network-connected speakers, add your Apple TV to a room in the Home app on your iOS or iPadOS device.

1. Make sure you're signed in with the same Apple ID on the Apple TV and the iOS or iPadOS device.

2. Open Settings ⚙️on Apple TV.

3. Go to Airplay > Room and follow the onscreen instructions to select the room where the Apple TV is located.

Select other rooms where you want audio to play

Do either of the following:

- Press and hold the Home ⬚button on the Siri Remote to open Control Center, select🔊, then select the room or rooms that correspond to your Airplay 2–enabled devices.

- While you're playing a song, podcast, or radio station, press and hold the Play/Pause button ▶‖on the Siri Remote, then select the room or rooms that correspond to your Airplay 2–enabled devices.

Ask Siri. Say something like:

  o "Play Troye Sivan in the kitchen and on the living room TV"

Stream from an iOS or iPadOS device to Apple TV

Do any of the following:

- *Mirror the screen of an iOS or iPadOS device on Apple TV:* On the iOS or iPadOS device, swipe to open Control Center, tap⌷▲⌷, then select Apple TV in the list of Airplay devices.

  To end mirroring, make sure Control Center is open on your device, tap⌷▲⌷, and then tap Stop Mirroring.

- *Stream video from an iOS or iPadOS device to Apple TV:* Start playing video on the iOS or iPadOS device, tap [▲]in the video window, then select Apple TV in   the list of Airplay devices.

Stream audio from an iOS or iPadOS device to Apple TV

- *From iOS or iPadOS Control Center:* Touch and hold the area above the Music playback controls, tap ⓐ, select   Apple TV in the list of devices, then tap Play/Pause ▶||(if the audio isn't already playing).

- *From the iOS or iPadOS Music app:* In Now Playing, tap ⓐ, select Apple TV in the list of devices, tap outside of the list, then tap Play/Pause ▶||(if the audio isn't already playing).

Stream from a   Mac to Apple TV

- *Mirror a Mac screen on Apple TV:* On the Mac, click [▲]in the Mac menu bar, then choose the name of the Apple TV you want to use.

  To end screen mirroring, click [▲]in the menu bar, then choose Turn Airplay Off.

- *Stream audio from a Mac to Apple TV:* Option-click the Sound icon in the Mac menu bar, then select Apple TV in the Output Device list.

Adjust Airplay and Home Kit settings

1. Open Settings on Apple TV.

2. Select Airplay and Home Kit, then do any of the following:

   o *Turn Airplay on or off:* Select Airplay to turn it on; select it again to turn it off.

   o *Allow access to Apple TV:* Select Allow Access, then follow the task below.

   o *Turn Conference Room Display on or off: Use iTunes in the Cloud:* Turn on Play Purchases from iCloud to tell Apple TV to stream the content from iTunes servers rather than over the local network from the Airplay-connected device.

   o *Fix a cropped Airplay display:* If your Airplay display appears cropped on Apple TV, turn on Airplay Display Underscan to show the entire image. If you see black bars around the image, turn this setting off.

44

○ *Select a Room:* Select Room, then choose the room where you keep your Apple TV.

Set who can use Airplay to stream content to Apple TV

1. Open Settings on Apple TV.

2. Select Airplay and Home Kit, then select Allow Access, and choose the following options:

   ○ *Everyone:* Everyone can stream content to your Apple TV.

   ○ *Anyone on the Same Network:* Anyone connected to your home network can stream content to your Apple TV

   ○ *Only People Sharing This Home:* Only people you've added to Home Sharing can stream content to your Apple TV.

   ○ *Require Password:* A password is required to Airplay to your Apple TV.

   ○ *Also Allow Nearby to Airplay:* Anyone close to your Apple TV can stream content to it.

Use Apple TV screen savers

Apple TV displays a screen saver after the screen is idle for a preset number of minutes.

The Aerial screen saver shows beautiful slow-motion videos of places around the world.

You can view information about the location shown, quickly switch to another location, and control how often Apple TV checks for and downloads new Aerial videos.

Activate the screen saver immediately

- On the Siri Remote, press and hold the MENU button to return to the Home screen, then press the MENU button again.

Use controls when the Aerial screen saver is active

On the Siri Remote, do any of the following:

- *Find out what location you're viewing:* Tap the Touch surface. On some screen savers, the location information changes with the viewing area so that specific landmarks are highlighted.

- *Go backward or forward to a different location:* Swipe left or right on the Touch surface.

Exit the screen saver

- When the screen saver is active, press the Touch surface on the Siri Remote to return to the app you were previously using.

Adjust screen saver settings

1. Open Settings ⚙ on Apple TV.

2. Go to General > Screen Saver, then do any of the following:

   o *Choose a different screen saver:* Select Type, then select the screen saver you want to use.

   o *Select which photos to display:* Many of the screen saver options display a slideshow of photos—these can be photos provided by Apple, or a collection of your own stored in iCloud. To choose which photos are used, select Type, then choose one of the photo-based screen saver types.

o *Change the Aerial screen saver download frequency:* Select Download New Video, then select an option.

o *Set the screen saver delay time:* Select Start After, then specify a number of minutes. This instructs Apple TV to automatically start the screen saver if the device has been idle for the specified duration.

o *Turn screen savers on or off during playback of music and podcasts:* Select Show during Music and Podcasts.

o *Preview a screen saver:* Select Preview.

Sleep or wake Apple TV

Apple TV is ready for you to watch at any time, and automatically goes to sleep after a preset period of inactivity.

Wake Apple TV from sleep

- Press the MENU, Home 🖵, Siri 🎤, or Play/Pause ▶II button on the Siri Remote.

  Apple TV wakes and displays whatever was last visible.

48

Set the delay before sleep starts

1. To set how long Apple TV waits before going to sleep, open Settings on Apple TV.

2. Go to General > Sleep After and choose an option.

Force Apple TV to sleep immediately

Do one of the following:

- On the Siri Remote, press and hold the Home button to open Control Center, then select Sleep.

- Open Settings on Apple TV, then select Sleep Now.

When you're done, you can also just shut off your television or audio/video receiver. Apple TV falls asleep after a period of inactivity.

About the Apple TV status light

The status light on the front of Apple TV indicates the following:

If Apple TV is	The status light
On	Glows

If Apple TV is	The status light
Off or in standby	Is off
Starting up	Flashes slowly
Accepting a command from the remote	Flashes once
Updating software	Flashes quickly

Chapter 3

Siri and Dictation

Talk to your Apple TV

Siri makes   interacting with Apple TV easy, fun, and informative. You can search for movies, TV shows, music, or apps; find actors or directors you like; control playback; open your apps; and even ask about sports,   weather,   and   stocks—no   matter   what's happening onscreen.

Siri doesn't talk back to you on Apple TV like it does on iPhone and other devices, but it'll carry out your request and display the results onscreen.

See a list of things you can ask Siri

- Press the Siri button 🎤on the Siri Remote.

Search and control Apple TV with your voice

- Press and hold the Siri button 🎤on the Siri Remote and start talking.

Siri understands a wide range of commands, and intuitively applies them to the current context whenever possible. To see some commands and queries that show   what Siri can do.

Dictate instead of type

Whenever you see a text   entry field, you can use your voice instead of using the onscreen keyboard.

- Press and hold the Siri   button 🎤on the Siri Remote and say the text you want to enter. You can even speak individual   characters—for example, when entering user names and passwords.

Search for content and apps on Apple TV

Siri on Apple TV helps you quickly find movies and TV shows to watch, and apps in the App Store to download. Siri can find   movies and TV shows based on a wide range of criteria—including title, topic, genre, actors, director, rating, age   appropriateness, and more. You can even ask to find "good" or "popular" results. For apps, you can search   by app name, developer, or category.

Search for movies, TV shows, and apps

Ask Siri. Say something   like:

- "What should I watch?"

- "Find 'Hidden   Figures'"

- "Play Episode 3 of Season 1 of 'Homeland'"

- "Show me   popular comedies"

- "What are the best baseball movies?"

- "Find Amy Adams movies"

- "Find   documentaries about cars"

- "Find me movies in 4K"

- "Find me   movies in HDR"

- "Watch great dramas"

- "Find me   some TV Shows that are good for kids"

- "Show PG-13 movies"

- "Find Crossey   Road"

- "Find weather apps"

- "What are some new sports apps?"

- "Find apps by   Activision"

Combine search terms

You can also combine   genres for movies and TV shows.

Ask Siri. Say something like:

- "Find me some funny horror movies"

- "Show me independent foreign films"

- "Search for crime documentaries"

Once you make an initial search, you can ask additional questions to zero in on exactly what you want to watch.

Search for free content

You can ask Siri to limit the search results to content that is immediately playable based on what you own and the services you already subscribe to.

Ask Siri. Say something like:

- "Find free kids' movies"

- "I want to watch 'Homeland' for free"

- "What are some free movies?"

When you search for a movie or TV show, Siri searches a wide range of apps to find exactly what you're looking for. If you request a specific title, Siri takes you directly to the detail page for that video. If there's more than one result, Siri displays search results for you to choose from or further refine your search.

Search within a specific app

You can search for items on YouTube by including "YouTube" in your Siri request (requires the YouTube app, available on the App Store for Apple TV). Siri automatically opens the YouTube app and adds your request to its search screen.

Ask Siri. Say something like:

- "Search for Coldplay on YouTube"

- "Show me crafts for kids on YouTube"

- "Search YouTube for Minecraft"

You can also search directly within many apps.

Search for podcasts

You can search specifically for podcasts by including "podcast" in your query.

Ask Siri. Say something like:

- "Get some funny podcasts"

- "Find podcasts about surfing"

- "Play 'Radiolab' podcast"

If you've subscribed to the selected podcast, Apple TV begins playing the current episode right away.

View search results on Apple TV

When you ask Siri to find movies, TV shows, actors or other subjects, the search results appear at the bottom of the screen.

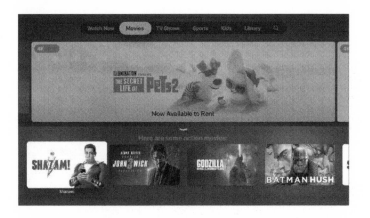

Select a search result

- Navigate to the result you want to open, then press the Touch surface on the Siri Remote.

  Information about the video appears, including a description, rating, cast, and which apps the video is available on. You can also play a trailer.

  If your query yields only one search result, Siri shows the details for that video.

View more information about a video

- Swipe down on the Touch surface of the Siri Remote to view more details about the video, including ratings and reviews.

Refine movie and TV show search results on Apple TV

You can refine a search for movies or TV shows by asking Siri for a subset of your initial search results. For example, if you ask Siri to show you Jason Bateman movies, you can then ask for a subset of them, such as:

Ask Siri. Say something like:

- Just show me the ones from this year"

- "Only the dramas"

- "Just the best ones"

Play live content on Apple TV

Some apps on Apple TV include live video streams featuring content like news or sports. You can use Siri to jump right into these live feeds.

Play live channels

Speak the name of the channel you want to watch and the live video stream immediately begins to play.

Ask Siri. Say something like:

- "Watch ESPN"

- "Turn on CBS News"

Play live sports

Ask Siri about a sports team, score, or schedule. If the game is available on a supported app, Siri takes you straight to the action.

Ask Siri. Say something like:

- "I want to watch the Braves game"

- "What hockey games are on?"

Select the Watch Live button to open the app and watch the game.

You can also ask about sports schedules in general.

Ask Siri. Say something like: "Who's playing baseball tonight?"

Siri shows you a list of all the relevant games, their start times and scores (if game has already started), and a Watch Now button if a supported app is currently airing the game.

Other things you can ask Siri on Apple TV

Siri can do much more than find a great show to watch or a great app to download. You can also use Siri to open apps on your Apple TV, control the playback of a video you're watching, learn more about the actors or director of a show, and much more.

Navigate Apple TV

You can use Siri to open an app or switch to another app.

Ask Siri. Say something like:

- "Open App Store"

- "Launch Showtime"

- "Play PBS KIDS Video"

- "Go to Photos"

Control video playback

When you're playing video content there are a number of commands you can use to control playback.

Ask Siri. Say something like:

- "Pause this"

- "Play from the beginning"

- "Skip forward 90 seconds"

- "Jump back 10 minutes"

- "Turn on closed captioning"

- "Turn on French subtitles"

- "What did she just say?"

    In this case, Apple TV skips back 15 seconds and temporarily turns on subtitles.

Get more information about a show

You can ask questions to get more information about a program you're watching.

Ask Siri. Say something like:

- "Who stars in this?"

- "Who directed this?"

- "What's this rated?"

- "When was this released?"

Play music

If you're an Apple Music subscriber, you can use Siri to play songs from Music.

Ask Siri. Say something like:

- "Play   'Sleek White Baby' by Punch Brothers"

- "Play the top ten hip-hop tracks"

- "Play the first Alabama Shakes album"

- "Add   'Uptown Funk' by Bruno Mars to my collection"

- "Play the live version of this song"

- "Play more like this"

Find an iOS, iPadOS, watchOS, or macOS device

If your other Apple devices (iOS, iPadOS, watchOS, or macOS) have the Find My feature enabled and are signed in using the same Apple ID that your Apple TV uses, you can ask Siri to trigger an audible alert on any of these devices. You're Apple TV and your device must be on the same network and nearby.

Ask Siri. Say something like:

- "Where is my iPhone?"

- "Ping my iPad"

- "Find Lisa's watch"

Control Home Kit products

If you're signed in on Apple TV with your Apple ID, you can ask Siri to control many Home Kit products, including lights, thermostats, shades, and more. When you're outside your home, you can use your iOS or iPadOS device with Siri and the Home app. You can change a setting, set a scene, get the status of a device, run automations, or get a list of devices.

Ask Siri. Say something like:

- "Dim the dining room lights to 50 percent"

- "Turn on the coffee maker"

- "How many outlets are in my apartment?"

- "Set the temperature to 72 degrees"

- "Are the upstairs lights on?"

- "Is the front door locked?"

- "Party"

- "Play this in the kitchen"

- "Goodnight"

- "I'm heading   out"

Note: You cannot control secure Home Kit-compatible products such as   door locks, motorized doors or windows, security systems, and garage doors from Apple TV. You must   use an iOS or iPad OS device to control to those devices.

Get general information

You can ask Siri about   other topics, like sports, weather, and stocks.

Ask Siri. Say something   like:

- "Who won the NBA Finals?"

- "Who are the Mavericks   playing tomorrow?"

- "How's the weather?"

- "What's the weather in   Vancouver?"

- "When is sunset in Paris?"

- "Where's the   NASDAQ today?"

- "How's Apple's stock?"

The results appear at   the bottom of the screen.

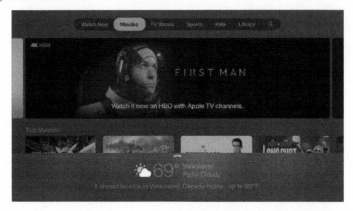

In some cases, you can swipe up on the Touch surface of the Siri Remote to reveal more information.

Use Siri to navigate Apple TV

Because Siri recognizes the names of onscreen labels, you can use your voice to navigate any screen on Apple TV. You can also use Siri to change settings.

Use Siri to navigate the interface of an app

- Press and hold the Siri button 🎤on the Siri Remote and say the name of an onscreen control—such as an item in the menu bar at the top of the iTunes Movies Store.

  Apple TV selects that control.

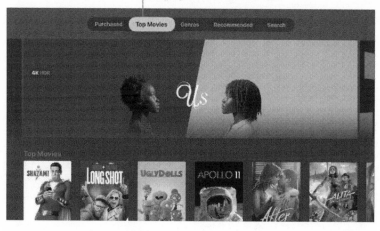

Speak the name of any onscreen control to highlight and select that item.

Use Siri to change settings

1. Open Settings ⚙ on Apple TV.

2. Press and hold the Siri button 🎤 on the Siri Remote and speak a command you see onscreen to open or activate that setting.

Use Siri dictation on Apple TV

Whenever you see an onscreen keyboard—such as when searching in a third party app or when entering a user name or password—you can speak the text instead of using the onscreen keyboard.

Speak text instead of typing it

- With a text entry field highlighted onscreen, press and hold the Siri button on the Siri Remote and speak whatever you want to enter in the text field.

Speak user names and passwords

- If a text field tells you to spell out characters instead of speaking words, press and hold the Siri button on the Siri Remote, then speak the letters, numbers, and symbols you want to enter.

  ○ Say "uppercase" to enter an uppercase letter.

  ○ Siri recognizes many domain names such as icloud.com, so they don't need to be spelled out.

  ○ You can use phonetic or military alphabet pronunciations, such as alpha, bravo, Charlie, delta for A, B, C, D, and so on.

  ○ You can use the special command "Clear" to delete the characters you just entered.

Clear applies only to characters spoken during the current Siri entry. For example, if you say "A, B, C," then release the Siri button, then press it again and say "1, 2, 3, clear," the numbers will be deleted but the letters will remain.

Turn dictation on or off

1. Open Settings on Apple TV.

2. Go to General > Dictation, then turn dictation on or off.

Turn Siri on or off on Apple TV

When you first set up Apple TV, you may be asked if you want to use Siri (depending on your country and language). You can change your mind at any time and turn Siri on or off.

Turn Siri on or off

1. Open Settings on Apple TV.

2. Go to General > Siri, then turn Siri on or off.

Chapter 4

Maximizing your Apple TV

Apple TV app at a glance

The Apple TV app  is the first place you go to start watching on your TV. It's all your TV, all in one place.

The Apple TV app is also available on all your screens, so you can take Apple TV wherever you go.

In the Apple TV app, you can:

- Continue playing your TV shows and movies from all your apps, all in one place

- Watch news and sports, and subscribe directly to Apple TV channels within the app (news, sports, and Apple TV channels are not available in all countries or regions)

- Get personalized recommendations based on your tastes and viewing history

- Explore the latest and recommended movies, TV shows, and collections, including Apple TV channels you haven't subscribed to yet

- Find and watch live sports (where available)

- Find and watch curated movies and TV shows for kids (not available in all countries or regions)

- Access your entire movie and TV show collection

The Apple TV app is available on Apple TV, iPhone, iPad, iPod touch, and Mac, as well as on some smart TVs.

Watch Now in the Apple TV app

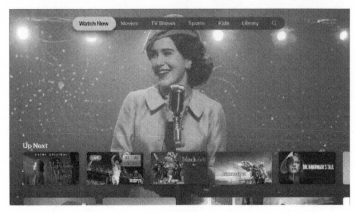

The Watch Now screen in the Apple TV app is the place to start watching movies, TV shows, news, and live sports. Find what you want to watch, add it to your Up Next list, and then start watching.

Browse content

1. Open the Apple TV app on Apple TV.

2. In the menu bar, swipe to Watch Now.

3. Swipe down to view recommended content—TV shows, movies, news, and sports, including collections hand-picked by experts as well as dedicated categories based on your viewing history.

Sports events in progress display the live score (to manage sports notifications,

Swipe to a category row (Hit Movies, for instance), then swipe right to see available content in that category.

4. Select an item in a category row to see its rating description, available viewing options, and purchase or rental information.

Play a movie, TV show, news program, or sports event

1. Find what you want to watch in the Apple TV app **tv**, then select it.

2. Do any of the following:

   ○ *Play the item or open it in a channel or app:* Select Play or Open In. If you haven't subscribed to the channel or app, follow the onscreen instructions.

   ○ *Buy or rent a movie:* Select Buy or Rent, then select the option you want and confirm your purchase or rental *Buy a TV show episode or season:* Select Buy, then select the option you want and confirm your purchase.

    ◦ *Watch a   sports event:* Select Live Now. For details,

During playback, press   the MENUbutton to return to the app that hosts the content you're watching. If you're watching a movie or TV   show, you'll see a menu to play from the beginning or access info and extras.

Press the Home   button ⌲when playing an item to return to the Watch Now screen in the Apple TV app.

Turn on picture-in-picture viewing

You can play movies   or TV shows from the Apple TV app 📺 in a small viewer that runs in the foreground while you browse other   content in the Apple TV app.

1. In the Apple TV app, choose a movie or TV show to begin   playing.

2. During playback, rest your finger on the Touch surface   of the Siri Remote to show the playback timeline, then swipe up and select the picture-in-picture ⊻ button   that appears.

On the Siri Remote, press the Home button ⌧ to see more options, then do any of the following:

- *Move the viewer to any corner of the screen:* Select the Move button ⬛⬛to move the viewer to the indicated corner of your screen. Select again to move it to the next corner, and so on.

- *Return to viewing full screen:* Select the Full-screen button ⬛.

- *Stop playback and close the viewer:* Select the Close button ⓧ.

3. On the Siri Remote, press the MENUbutton to continue watching in picture-in-picture mode.

See what's up next

The Up Next row displays content you've already started to watch or plan to watch.

- In the Watch Now screen of the Apple TV app , navigate to the Up Next row, then swipe left or right to see shows you've recently watched or added to Up Next.

  Shows and movies appear in the order you're most likely to want to watch them. For example, when a TV episode is finished, the next episode automatically appears in Up Next. And if you've already caught up on a show, whenever a new episode becomes available, it immediately shows up in the beginning of the Up Next row.

  If your favorite sports team is playing on an app you're signed in to, such as ESPN, the live game in progress appears in Up Next. Alerts appear onscreen if the game is close so that you can quickly switch to the action. To manage sports notifications, if you have an iPad or iPhone and are signed in with the same account you use for Apple TV, your viewing progress and episode selection stay in sync in the Apple TV app on those devices. For example, you can start watching a show on your Apple TV and finish watching it on iPad, or vice versa.

Add a movie, TV show, or sports event to Up Next

1. On the Watch Now screen in the Apple TV app **tv**, select an item to see its rating, description, available viewing options, and purchase or rental information.

2. Select Add to Up Next.

   A notification appears indicating the item is added.

Remove an item from Up Next

Do either of the following:

- Select In Up Next. (If you don't see the in up next button, first select the item in the Up Next row.)

- Highlight the item in the Up Next row, press and hold the Touch surface of the Siri Remote, then select Remove from Up Next.

Start watching from Up Next

- In the Apple TV app , highlight an item in the Up Next row, then press the Touch surface of the Siri Remote to start playing it.

When you ask Siri to play a TV show, Apple TV automatically starts the next episode you haven't seen, whether it's the middle of season 1, or last night's episode.

Movies in the Apple TV app

The Movies screen in the Apple TV app  contains great new movie content across Apple TV channels and apps, including those you haven't yet installed or subscribed to, as well as the latest releases. You can discover recommendations based on your taste, or browse the hottest new releases, collections, and other offers.

Once you find a movie you want to watch, you can choose how to watch it if it's available on multiple channels and apps. If the movie's available to start playing immediately, you'll get the default channel or app that lets you watch it in the highest-quality version.

Browse featured and recommended movies

1. Open the Apple TV app on Apple TV.

2. In the menu bar, swipe to Movies, then browse featured movies, genres, and collections.

   Recommendations appear based on your tastes or past viewing or purchase/rental history (If you like Shrek 2, for example).

3. Select a movie to see previews, ratings, descriptions, and viewing information.

Pick a movie to watch

When you select a movie, a new screen appears with ratings, descriptions, and viewing information, including all of the ways you can watch the movie on Apple TV. After a few seconds, a free preview begins playing in the background.

1. In the Apple TV app , do any of the following:

   ○ *Watch a free preview:* If a preview is available, it automatically begins playing in the background. Swipe up on the Touch surface of the Siri Remote to watch the preview in full screen.

   ○ *Play the movie:* If the movie is already available to you to watch as a purchase or an indicated channel or app, select play to start watching it immediately.

   ○ *Buy or rent the movie:* Select Buy or Rent, then select the option you want and confirm your purchase or rental.

In some regions, you can rent movies. You have 30 days to begin watching a rented movie. After you start watching it, you can play it as many times as you want within 48 hours. During the rental period, you can download the rented movie on one device at any given time and also stream it on another. For example, you can start watching a movie downloaded on your iPhone, then finish watching it later on your Apple TV. Once your time is up, the movie is no longer available.

- ○ *Open the movie in an available TV channel:* Select Play.

- ○ *Open the movie in another app:* Select "Open In", then select an app. If an app isn't immediately available, follow the onscreen instructions to install it and connect to it. Some apps may require a subscription.

- ○ *Add an item to Up Next:* If you want to watch the movie later, select add to Up

Next to add it to Up Next in the Watch Now screen.

- o *Remove an item from Up Next:* Select in up Next.

- o *Go to the next movie in the category you're browsing:* Swipe right or left. You can also press the MENUbutton on the Siri Remote to go back to the Movies screen.

2. To get more information, scroll down to highlight a row or item, then do any of the following:

- o *Watch additional trailers:* Scroll left or right in the Additional Trailers row, then select a trailer.

- o *Browse related movies:* Scroll left or right in the related row, then select a movie.

- o *Preview Extras:* Select to preview additional menu items and video extras available when you purchase the movie from Apple.

- o *Explore cast and crew:* Scroll left or right in the Cast & Crew row, then select a person to see biographical information and associated movies and TV shows.

○ *See viewing options:* Scroll left or right in the How to Watch row to see all of the ways to watch the movie on Apple TV, including pricing options to buy or rent, or the available Apple TV channels or apps.

Some content and apps are available with a subscription. To sign up, select the item and follow the sign-up process using your Apple ID. If you haven't installed the app yet, you'll be prompted to download it from the App Store.

Other content may be available to you with your cable or satellite subscription. If this is your first time using an app that requires a cable or satellite subscription, you may need to enter your TV provider credentials.

○ *Get more information:* Scroll to the bottom of the screen to see ratings, descriptions, and other information.

When you buy or rent a movie, it automatically plays in the highest-quality format available for your Apple TV, including high-definition (HD) and 4K resolution formats. These videos might also feature high dynamic range (HDR) in HDR10 or Dolby Vision, and Dolby Atmos.

TV Shows in the Apple TV app

The TV Shows screen in the Apple TV app ![tv] contains all of your favorite TV shows, news, and Apple TV channels, including recommendations based on your taste and viewing history.

Once you find a TV show you want to watch, you can choose how to watch it if it's available on multiple channels and apps. If it's available to start playing immediately, you'll get the default channel or app that lets you watch it in the highest-quality version.

Browse featured and recommended TV shows

1. Open the Apple TV app on Apple TV.

2. In the menu bar, swipe to TV Shows, then browse featured TV shows, news, genres, and collections.

   Recommendations appear based on your tastes or past viewing or purchase/rental history (If you like The Daily Show, for example).

3. Select a TV show to see previews, ratings, descriptions, and viewing information.

Pick a TV show to watch

When you select a TV show, a new screen appears with ratings, descriptions, and viewing information, including all of the ways you can watch the TV show on Apple TV. If you're buying episodes, you can select individual episodes or an entire season.

1. In the Apple TV app tv , do any of the following:

- *Play the TV show:* If the TV show is already available to you to watch as a purchase or on an indicated channel or app, select play to start watching it immediately.

- *Buy an episode or season:* Select "Buy from [price]," then select the option you want and confirm your purchase.

- *Open the TV show in an available channel:* Select Play.

- *Open the TV show in another app:* Select "Open In", then select an app. If an app isn't immediately available, follow the onscreen instructions to install it and connect to it. Some apps may require a subscription.

- *Add an item to Up Next:* If you want to watch the TV show later, select add to Up Next to add it to Up Next in the Watch Now screen.

- ○ *Remove an item from Up Next:* Select in up Next.

- ○ *Go to the next TV show in the category you're browsing:* Swipe right or left. You can also press the MENUbutton on the Siri Remote to go back to the TV Shows screen.

2. To get more information, scroll down to highlight a row or item, then do any of the following:

- ○ *Browse seasons and episodes:* Select an episode, or select a season, then browse episodes. When you select an episode, you'll be able to pick which channel or app you want to use.

- ○ *Browse related TV shows:* Scroll left or right in the related row, then select a TV show.

- ○ *Explore cast and crew:* Scroll left or right in the Cast & Crew row, then select a person to see biographical information and associated movies and TV shows.

- ○ *See viewing options:* Scroll left or right in the How to Watch row to see all of the ways to watch the TV show on Apple TV, including pricing options to buy, or the available Apple TV channels or apps.

Some content and apps are available with a subscription. To sign up, select the item and follow the sign-up process using your Apple ID. If you haven't installed the app yet, you'll be prompted first to download it from the App Store.

Other content may be available to you with your cable or satellite subscription. If this is your first time using an app that requires a cable or satellite subscription, you may need to enter your TV provider credentials *get more information:* Scroll to the bottom of the screen to see ratings, descriptions, and other information.

Sports in the Apple TV app

The Sports screen in the Apple TV app  gives you immediate access to a wide array of live and scheduled sports events (not available in all countries or regions).

You can see games in progress with up-to-the-minute scores, or browse upcoming games and add them to Up Next. You can also customize Sports to be notified about upcoming events and see live scores for your favorite teams.

Browse and watch live sports

1. Open the Apple TV app on Apple TV.

2. In the menu bar, swipe to Sports, then explore featured games, or browse by sport or category.

3. To start watching, select a sports event in progress, then select Live Now or Open In. If

you haven't subscribed to the channel or app, follow the onscreen instructions.

Add an upcoming event to Up Next

1. In the Sports screen of the Apple TV app , swipe to highlight an event, then press the Touch surface of the Siri Remote to select it.

   The event's scheduled time, network, and other information are shown.

2. Select Add to Up Next.

   The event is placed in the Up Next row of the Watch Now screen.

Remove an item from Up Next

- In the Sports screen of the Apple TV app , select the event to see more information, then select In up Next to remove it from the queue.

Pick your favorite teams to follow

You can pick your favorite teams and then receive a notification when they're about to play.

1. In the Sports screen of the Apple TV app , select Your Favorite Teams, then scroll to a category in the list.

2. Highlight your team, then press the Touch surface of the Siri Remote to add it.

To remove a team, select it in Favorites, then select Remove.

Kids in the Apple TV app

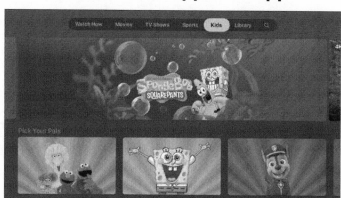

The Kids screen in the Apple TV app ▇tv is a curated collection of movies and TV shows just for kids. You can browse by age or other categories.

Browse content for kids

1. Open the Apple TV app ▇tv on Apple TV.

2. In the menu bar, swipe to Kids, then browse featured movies, TV shows, and collections.

3. Select an item to see ratings, descriptions, and purchase or rental information.

Play a movie or TV show

When you find what you want to watch, select it, then choose from any of the options that appear:

- *Play the item or open it in a channel or app:* Select Play or Open In. If you haven't subscribed to the channel or app, follow the onscreen instructions.

- *Buy or rent a movie:* Select Buy or Rent, then select the option you want and confirm your purchase or rental.

- *Buy a TV show episode or season:* Select Buy, then select the option you want and confirm your purchase.

Library in the Apple TV app

The Library screen in the Apple TV app [tv] includes your purchases and rentals, organized by category.

90

Browse your Library in the Apple TV app

1. Open the Apple   TV app on Apple TV.

2. In the menu bar, swipe to Library, then browse items, or select a   category or genre to filter items.

Play a movie or TV show

- When you find what   you want to watch, select it, then select Play.

Search in the Apple TV app

The Search screen in the Apple TV app lets you find TV shows and movies by   title, cast, or crew.

Search for items in the Apple TV app

1. Open the Apple TV app on Apple TV.

2. In the menu bar, swipe to Search Q, then do any of the following:

   ○ Browse items that appear in trending categories.

   ○ Enter a search term in the field.

   Tip: To dictate instead of type, press and hold the Siri button 🎤on the Siri Remote and speak.

3. Select an item to see ratings, descriptions, and purchase or rental information.

You can also use Siri for search at any time.

Adjust Apple TV app settings

You can choose what appears in the Apple TV app 📺, including Apple TV channels and apps, live scores, notifications, play history, and items in Up Next.

Adjust settings for the Apple TV app

1. Open Settings ⚙ on Apple TV.

2. Go to Apps > TV, then do any of the following:

   ○ *Use your play history for personalized recommendations and Up Next:* Turn on Use Play History.

o *See live sports scores in Up Next:* Turn on Show Sports Scores.

o *Get   Game   Start   and   Close   Game notifications for games you've added to Up Next:* Turn on Games in Up Next.

o *Get notifications about recommended sports and events:* Turn on Exciting Games.

o *Set which Apple TV channels and apps share content with the Apple TV app:* Select an app from the list to turn it on or off.

o *Remove   information   about   what   you've watched (which is synced with the Apple TV app on other devices):* Select Clear Play History. This also removes TV shows and movies from Up Next.

Chapter 5

Music

Apple Music app at a glance

Use the Apple Music app [♫] on Apple TV to enjoy music in the following ways:

- Access millions of songs and thousands of ad-free music videos on Apple Music (requires a subscription). Discover Apple Music recommendations based on your tastes, or browse the hottest new music and recommendations from music experts Listen to dozens of hand-curated, ad-free radio stations and Beats 1 radio brought to you by Apple Music.

- Listen to music from your Cloud Music Library, including music you add from Apple Music, your iTunes Store purchases, songs uploaded from your computer, and your iTunes Match library.

To join Apple Music, go to the Apple Music app on an iOS or iPadOS device, or the Apple Music app on a Mac running macOS Catalina, or iTunes on a PC or Mac running macOS Mojave or earlier.

Note: In some cases an Apple ID is required. Services and features are not available in all countries or regions, and features may vary by area. You can play Apple Music and Radio tracks on only one device at a time unless you have an Apple Music Family Membership, which lets you play music on multiple devices. If you end your Apple Music membership, you can no longer stream Apple Music tracks or play Apple Music tracks saved for offline play.

You can also use Apple TV to stream music that's in the Apple Music app on your Mac, iOS device, or iPadOS device (or in the iTunes library on a Mac with macOS Mojave or earlier installed).

Now Playing: Control music   playback on Apple TV

No matter where you are in the Apple Music app 🎵 , you can select a song, then   press the Touch surface to start playing it.

Once a song starts playing, it   appears in Now Playing.

The song continues to play even if you leave Music, but it stops if you begin playing   video or audio in another app.

Go to Now Playing

- Open Music 🎵 on Apple   TV, then swipe to Now Playing.

  Songs adjacent to the   currently playing one appear in the Now Playing queue. A timeline also appears showing elapsed   and remaining time. When the timeline is active, you can also press the Touch surface to play or   pause the song.

  Once you start playing a song, the screen changes to show just the currently   playing song. Press the MENU button to return to Now Playing.

Control music during playback

1. With the Now Playing screen open on Apple TV, swipe down to the song you want to play, then press the Touch surface of the Siri Remote to begin playing it.

   The Now Playing screen changes to show just the currently playing song.

2. Do any of the following on the Siri Remote:

   o *Pause or play:* Press the Play/Pause button ▶︎‖or press the Touch surface.

   o *Go back to the beginning or skip to the next song:* Press the left or right side of the Touch surface to restart the current song or skip to the start of the next song.

   o *Rewind or fast forward:* Press left or right and hold to rewind or fast forward during playback. Release to resume playback.

   o *Move to a specific point in the song:* Press the Touch surface to pause the song and reveal the play head, then swipe left or right to move backward or forward on the timeline. Press the Touch surface again to resume playback.

    o *Go back to Now Playing:* Press the MENU button.

Select other rooms where you want audio to play

1. Do either of the following:

       o With the Now Playing screen open on Apple TV, swipe up to the controls at the top of the screen; swipe left and select 📡.

       o Press and hold the Play/Pause ▶︎||button on the Siri Remote.

2. Select the room or rooms.

   Ask Siri. Say something like:

       o "Play Troye Sivan in the kitchen and on the living room TV"

Quickly add a song to your library

- With the Now Playing screen open on Apple TV, swipe up and select the Add button ⊕.

View a song's lyrics

You can view a song's lyrics if you're a member of Apple Music.

1. With the Now Playing screen open on Apple TV, swipe up and select the Lyrics button .

2. Swipe up and down in the lyrics to find a lyric you want to hear, then press the Touch surface of the Siri Remote.

As you swipe up and down, a button appears to indicate the specific time where each lyric can be heard in the song's timeline. Press the Touch surface of the Siri Remote to begin playback from that point.

To turn lyrics off, swipe up and select the Lyrics button at the top of the screen.

Note: The Lyrics button won't appear if lyrics aren't available for the currently playing song.

See more options

- With the Now Playing screen open on Apple TV, swipe up and select the more button ⬤at the top of the screen. Depending on the song, you may be able to:

  - Go to the album

  - Go to the artist

  - Add the song to or delete the song from your library

  - View the song lyrics

  - Add the song to a playlist

  - Play the song next

  - Start a custom radio station from the song

  - Flag the song as one you love or dislike

  - Change your speaker settings

Repeat a song or songs

- With the Now Playing screen open on Apple TV, swipe up and select the Repeat button ⬤at the top of the screen.

  To repeat the current song, select the Repeat button again.

Shuffle songs

- With the Now Playing screen open on Apple TV, swipe up and select the Shuffle button ⤨at the top of the screen.

Library: Browse and play your music on Apple TV

The Library screen in the Apple Music app 🎵 includes any Apple Music content and playlists you added, iTunes Store purchases and playlists you created, and music you make available through iTunes Match.

Note: You cannot sign up for iTunes Match on Apple TV. You must subscribe to iTunes Match in the Apple Music app on an iOS device, an iPadOS device, or a Mac with macOS Catalina; or in iTunes on a Mac with macOS Mojave or earlier.

Browse and play music from your library

1. Open Music 🎵 on Apple TV.

2. Swipe to Library, then select an option in the list to display your music in categories such as Recently Added, Playlists, Artists, Albums, Songs, and more.

3. Select a song to play it.

Browse playlists

1. Open Music on Apple TV, then swipe to Library.

2. Select Playlists, then select one of your playlists.

3. Select a song to play it.

   In addition to playlists you create on the Now Playing screen, Playlists includes playlists you added from Apple Music, as well as those shared with you.

Shuffle songs

1. Open Music on Apple TV, then swipe to Library.

2. Do either of the following:

   ○ *Play all of your library in random order:* Select Shuffle All at the top of the list.

   ○ *Play an album in random order:* Select the album, then select the Shuffle button ⤮.

   Ask Siri. Say something like:

   ○ "Play Bastille shuffled"

   ○ "Play 'More Rain' shuffled"

See more options

1. Open Music 🎵 on Apple TV, then swipe to Now
   Playing.

2. Press the Touch surface on the Siri Remote,
   then swipe up and select the more button ⬤ at
   the top of the screen to see more options.

   Playlists you create on Apple TV are added to
   your Cloud Music Library and appear on all your
   devices.

For You: Listen to personalized music on Apple TV

For you appears in the Apple Music app 🎵 menu bar if
you're a member of Apple Music. Apple Music
suggests curated playlists and albums, based on your
specific tastes.

When you're an Apple Music member, you can see
music your friends are listening to by following them.
You can also see the playlists they've shared and the
music they listen to most often. Likewise, your
followers can see your shared playlists and the music
you often listen to.

Browse music custom-picked for you

1. Open Music 🎵 on Apple TV, then swipe to For You.

2. Highlight an album or playlist, then press the Touch surface to view it.

3. Select a song to play it.

   If you find a recommendation you don't care for, press and hold the Touch surface of the Siri Remote, then select Dislike.

Add a song, album, or playlist to your library

1. Open Music 🎵 on Apple TV, then swipe to For You.

2. Select a song, album, or playlist.

3. Do any of the following:

   ○ Press and hold the Touch surface of the Siri Remote, then select Add to Library.

   ○ Select the Add button ╋.

   ○ In Now Playing, select the more button ⬤, then select Add to Library.

The playlist remains in your library, and updates automatically if the playlist changes.

Remove a song, album, or playlist from your library

1. Open Music 🎵 on Apple TV, then swipe to For You.

2. Select a song, album, or playlist.

3. Do one of the following:

   ○ Press and hold the Touch surface of the Siri Remote, then select Delete from Library.

   ○ In Now Playing, select the more button 🔘, then select Delete from Library.

Tell Music what you love

To help improve future recommendations, do one of the following in Music 🎵 on Apple TV:

• Press and hold the Touch surface of the Siri Remote, then select Love.

- In Now Playing, select the more button ●●●, then select Love.

Get more songs by this artist

In Music 🎵 on Apple TV, do one of the following:

- Swipe to a song, press and hold the Touch surface on the Siri Remote, then select Go to Artist.

- Select the Go to Artist button 🎤 while viewing an album's contents.

- In Now Playing, select the more button ●●●, then select Go to Artist.

Get more song, album, or playlist options

In the Music 🎵 on Apple TV, do one of the following:

- *Get album or playlist options:* While viewing an item's contents, select the more button ●●● to add music to the Up Next queue, create a station based on the currently selected music, add the playlist's songs to your own playlist, or rate whether you love or dislike the item.

- *Get song options:* Highlight a song in a playlist, then press and hold the Touch surface to see more options. Depending on the song, you can choose to view the album or artist, add it to your library, add it to a playlist, play it next, create a station, view lyrics, flag it as a song you love or dislike, or change your speakers.

Browse: Discover Apple Music on Apple TV

Browse appears in the Apple Music app 🎵 menu bar if you're a member of Apple Music. Browse showcases the best recommendations from music experts.

Browse and play expert recommendations

1. Open Music 🎵 on Apple TV, then swipe to browse.

2. Swipe down to see a menu of Browse categories.

3. Do any of the following:

   o *Browse new music:* Select the New Music category at the top of the screen.

   o *Fit the music to the mood:* Select the Curated Playlists category, then browse Activities & Moods.

107

○ *See what's hot:* Select the Top Charts category, where you can view top songs, top albums, and other popular content.

○ *Hear music handpicked by experts:* Select the Genres category, then choose a genre.

4. Highlight a featured album, artist, music video, or playlist, then press the Touch surface of the Siri Remote to view it.

5. Select a song to play it, or press and hold the Touch surface to show a menu with more options.

Depending on the song, you can create a station, add it to a playlist or your library, or remove it from your library.

Ask Siri. Say something like:

○ "Add this to my collection"

○ "Create a radio station based on this song"

Videos: Watch music videos on Apple TV

Videos appears in the Apple Music app menu bar if you're a member of Apple Music. Videos includes the best and hottest new music videos and video playlists.

Browse and play music videos

1. Open Music on Apple TV, then swipe to Videos.

2. Swipe down to see a menu of Videos categories.

3. Do any of the following:

   ○ *Browse featured items and playlists:* Swipe left or right to browse the items at the top of the screen.

   ○ *See what's hot:* Swipe down to New Music Videos, then swipe left or right to browse items.

   ○ *Browse curated playlists:* Swipe down to Music Video Playlists, then swipe left or right to browse playlists.

   ○ *Browse by genre:* Swipe down to any genre category, then swipe left or right to browse items.

4. Highlight a music video or playlist, then press the Touch surface of the Siri Remote to view it.

5. Select a song to play it, or press and hold the Touch surface to show a menu with more options.

Depending on the song, you can add it to a playlist or your library, or remove it from your library.

Ask Siri. Say something like:

   o "Add this to my collection"

Radio: Listen to stations on Apple TV

The Radio screen in the Apple Music app offers the always-on Beats 1, featuring top DJs playing today's best music, as well as a collection of stations based on different genres. Stations created by experts provide a great way to explore and enjoy new music. You can also create your own custom stations, based on your pick of artist, song, or genre.

Listen to Beats 1 radio

1. Open Music on Apple TV.

2. Swipe down to see a menu of Radio categories.

3. Swipe to Beats 1, then select Listen Now to listen to live radio, or browse and select to play previously recorded shows.

Listen to stations

1. Open Music ♫ on Apple TV.

2. Swipe down to see a menu of Radio categories.

3. Swipe to Feature or Stations.

4. Select a station to start listening.

Start a station

1. Open Music ♫ on Apple TV.

2. Swipe to Now Playing, then swipe down to see the currently playing song.

3. Do one of the following:

    o Press and hold the Touch surface and select Create Station.

    o Press the Touch surface to show additional controls, select the more button ⦁⦁⦁, then select Create Station.

      Newly created stations appear in the Featured category of the Radio screen.

Ask Siri. Say something like:

• "Play the radio station 'Pure Pop'"

- "Create a radio station based on this song"

Search: Find music on Apple TV

You can find and add music for your Apple TV in a variety of ways.

Find music in your library

1. Open Music ♫ on Apple TV, then select Search in the menu bar.

2. Swipe down to activate the onscreen keyboard.

3. Enter a song, album, playlist, artist, compilation, or genre, then select Library.

Search Apple Music

1. Open Music ♫ on Apple TV, then select Search in the menu bar.

2. Swipe down to select a trending search—or use the onscreen keyboard to enter a song, album, playlist, artist, curator, music video, activity, radio station, or genre, then select All Apple Music.

Use Siri to find music

Do one of the following:

112

- In the Search   screen, highlight the text entry field, press and hold the Siri button on the Siri Remote, then   speak.

  For example, say the name of the artist, album, or song you're looking   for.

- From anywhere else on Apple TV, press and hold the Siri button on   the Siri Remote and say the name of an artist, album, or song you're looking for.

Control music with Siri on Apple TV

You can use Siri to control   music playback on Apple TV.

Use Siri to control music playback

- Press and hold the Siri button 🎤 on the Siri Remote, then speak a command.

  Use Siri voice commands to do the following:

  - *Search for music:* Say the name of the artist, album, or song you're looking for.

  - *Play or pause music:* Say "Play music." To pause, say "Pause," "Pause music," or "Stop." You can also say "Next song" or "Previous song."

  - *Play an album, artist, song, playlist, or radio station:* Say "Play" followed by the name of the artist, album, song, playlist, or station that you want to play. If Siri doesn't find what you asked for, be more specific. For example, say "Play the radio station 'Pure Pop'" rather than saying "Play 'Pure Pop.'"

  - *Play music in random order:* Say the name of the artist ("Play Bastille shuffled") or album ("Play 'More Rain' shuffled") that you'd like to hear in random order.

114

○ *Play similar music:* While music is playing, say "Play more songs like this one" or "Create a radio   station based on this song."

○ *Browse   Apple   Music   (Apple   Music membership required):* You can play any Apple Music track by title ("Play 'Uptown Funk' by Bruno Mars"), by artist ("Play Alabama Shakes"), by chart ("Play the top song from March 1989"), or by version ("Play the live version of it").

○ *Add music from   Apple Music to your collection (Apple   Music   membership required):* Say, for example, "Add 'Sleek White Baby' by Punch Brothers to Library" or, while playing something, say "Add this to my collection."

Adjust music   settings on Apple TV

There are a few settings you can use to control how music is played back on Apple TV.

Adjust music settings

1. Open Settings on Apple TV.

2. Go to Apps > Music and do any of the following:

- *Automatically add to your library any Apple Music songs you add to playlists:* Turn on Add Playlist Songs to Library.

- *Normalize the sound level of your music:* Turn on Sound Check.

- *Share music played on Apple TV with your followers on Apple Music:* Turn on Use Listening History. When turned on, this setting also influences the recommendations you get on the For You screen.

Show the screen saver while listening to music

1. Open Settings on Apple TV.

2. Go to General > Screen Saver and turn on Show during Music and Podcasts.

Find games in the Apple Arcade

Apple Arcade is an ad-free, subscription-based gaming service. Use the Arcade app to sign up for, browse, and download games on Apple TV.

All of the games in Apple Arcade on Apple TV are also available in Apple Arcade on other devices, so for example, you can start playing a game on your iPhone and pick up where you left off later on a bigger TV screen connected to your Apple TV. (Available on iPhone and iPod touch with iOS13, Mac with Catalina, and iPad with iPadOS.)

You can also use the Sony PlayStation Dual Shock 4, Microsoft Xbox Wireless Controller with Bluetooth, and MFi-compatible game controllers to play games. For more information, *Note:* Game controllers work with select games and are sold separately. Availability may vary by country.

Sign up for Apple Arcade

1. Open the Arcade app  on Apple TV.

2. Follow the onscreen instructions to sign in with your Apple ID to get started.

Browse the Arcade app

1. Open the Arcade app on Apple TV.

2. Swipe down to view recommended content, including collections hand-picked by experts as well as dedicated categories based on your gaming history.

3. Swipe to a category row (Games for you, for instance), then swipe right to see available content in that category.

4. Select an item in a category row to see its rating description, available options, and other information.

Search the Arcade app

1. Open the Arcade app on Apple TV.

2. Select the Search button $\mathcal{Q}$in the upper-right corner.

3. Enter a search term to find apps by name.

Download a game

1. Find a game you want to play in the Arcade app
   , then select it.

2. Follow the onscreen instructions to try it or download it.

While a game is downloading or updating, its icon appears on the Home screen with a progress indicator.

Tip: If you set up Family Sharing, your family organizer can review purchases made by other family members under the age of 18. For example, if Ask to Buy is set for younger family members (configured in System Preferences on a Mac running macOS Catalina, in iTunes on a Mac running macOS Mojave or earlier, or on an iOS or iPadOS device), then when those members try to make a purchase, a message is sent to the family organizer asking for approval.

Chapter 6

Photos

Apple TV Photos app at a glance

The Photos app  lets you enjoy your pictures and videos on the big screen. You can use the following services to view the photos and videos from your iCloud account:

- *ICloud Photos:* iCloud Photos automatically stores your full-resolution photos and videos in iCloud. You can access iCloud Photos from any device using the same Apple ID. You can't edit photos and videos on Apple TV, but you can use the Photos app on other iOS and iPadOS devices and Mac computers to edit them and have those changes automatically update on Apple TV and all of your other devices.

- *Memories:* You can view all the memories created on your iOS or iPadOS device, or Mac. You can also adjust playback settings, see all the photos and videos that make up each collection, and more. *My Photo Stream:* My Photo Stream automatically uploads new photos taken on an iOS or iPadOS device to your other devices that use My Photo Stream, including Apple TV.

- *Shared Albums:* You can view albums of photos and videos shared from another iOS or iPadOS device or Mac using Shared Albums, or view other people's shared albums if you're subscribed.

Note: Photos shared using Home Sharing on your computer appear only in the Computers app 🖼️, not in the Photos app 🌸.

Turn on access to photos from iCloud

1. Open Settings ⚙️ on Apple TV.

2. Go to Users and Accounts > iCloud, then turn on iCloud Photos or Shared Albums.

View iCloud Photos on Apple TV

In the Photos app 🌸, photos, Live Photos, and videos from your iCloud Photos appear in the Photos category in the menu bar. Your iCloud Photos albums appear in the Albums category in   the menu bar.

View your iCloud Photos items

1. Open the Photos app on Apple TV, then swipe to the Photos category in the menu bar.

2. Swipe up or down on the Touch surface to scroll through the items, which are organized by date and location.

   Tip: If you have a large library with years of photos, rest your finger on the right side of the Touch surface to activate a scrolling timeline. Then swipe up or down to the year you want to view.

3. To view and scroll through full-screen photos, select a photo, then   swipe left or right.

View your iCloud Photos albums

In Albums, you can see all of the albums created on your iOS or iPadOS devices, or Mac, such as Favorites or Selfies.

1. Open the Photos app on Apple TV, then swipe to the   Albums category in the menu bar.

2. Select an album, then swipe left or right on the Touch surface to scroll through the photos.

3. To view and scroll through full-screen photos, select a photo, then swipe left or right.

View photo memories on Apple TV

The Memories screen in the Photos app 🌸 automatically arranges photos and videos you haven't seen or thought about in a while. Trips, events, and moments are presented in a gallery and as a short movie that you can watch on the big screen.

To get memories on your Apple TV, you need to have photos and videos on another iOS device, iPadOS device, or Mac linked to the same iCloud Photos account. The best memories created on those devices will automatically become available on your Apple TV.

You can't create or edit memories on Apple TV, but you can adjust playback settings such as mood and duration.

Browse your memories

1. Open the Photos app 🌸 on Apple TV, then swipe to the Memories category in the menu bar.

2. Select a memory, then do any of the following:

- o *Watch the movie:* Select the movie at the top of the screen.

- o *View individual photos and videos from the movie:* Swipe down on the Touch surface to scroll through a summary of photos and videos from the movie. Select a photo or video to view it full-screen. Select Show More to see more items.

- o *View a map of locations where the photos or videos were taken:* Swipe down on the Touch surface, then select the map shown in Places. Swipe up, down, left, or right to pan the map, or press the Play/Pause button ▶︎‖to access additional controls for zooming in or out, moving the map, or changing selections.

- o *View photo collections of people that appear in the memory:* Swipe down on the Touch surface, then select any person shown in People.

◦ *View related memories:* Swipe down on the Touch surface to browse additional memories. Select a memory to open it.

◦ *Add a memory to your Favorite Memories album:* Swipe down on the Touch surface to the bottom of the screen, then select Add to Favorite Memories. The Favorite Memories album can be found in the Albums category of the Photos app.

◦ *Set a memory as the Apple TV screen saver:* Swipe down on the Touch surface to the bottom of the screen, then select Set as Screen saver

Play a memory and adjust playback settings

1. In the Memories category of the Photos app on Apple TV, select a movie to play it.

2. During playback, swipe down to show the Info pane, then do any of the following:

◦ *Change the mood:* Swipe to Mood, then swipe down and select the mood you prefer.

o *Change the duration:* Swipe to Duration, then swipe down and select Short, Medium, or Long.

o *Access audio controls:* Swipe to Audio, then swipe down and select the option you prefer.

Delete, block, or add a memory   to favorites

- In the Memories category of the Photos app on Apple TV, highlight a memory, press and hold the Touch surface of the Siri Remote, then select any of the   following:

  o *Add to (or Remove from) Favorite Memories:* Add or remove the memory from the Favorite Memories album found in the Albums category of the Photos app.

  o *Delete Memory:* Permanently delete the memory on Apple TV and on all devices connected to your iCloud Photos account.

  o *Block Memory:* Block memories of that particular day or place on Apple TV and on all devices connected to your iCloud Photos account.

View shared   photos and albums on Apple TV

In the Photos app ⚘ , photos and videos you shared with others, or that others shared with you, appear in the Shared category in the menu bar.

Browse and view shared photos

1. Open the Photos app ⚘ on Apple TV, then swipe to the Shared category in the menu bar.

   Note: If you don't see the Shared category, go to Settings > Users and Accounts > iCloud and turn on Shared Albums.

2. To browse your photos, do any of the following:

   o *Browse your most recent shared photos:* Select Activity, then swipe left or right on the Touch surface to scroll through the photos.

   o *View your My Photo Stream album:* Select Photo Stream in My Albums, then swipe left or right on the Touch surface to scroll through the photos.

   o *View a shared album:* Select an album in My Albums, then swipe left or right on the Touch surface to scroll through the photos.

To view a list of people who are subscribed to this shared album, select People.

3. To view and scroll through photos full screen, select a photo, then swipe left or right.

View comments and like photos in a shared album

1. Open the Photos app on Apple TV, then swipe to the Shared category in the menu bar.

   Note: If you don't see the Shared category, go to Settings > Users and Accounts > iCloud and turn on Shared Albums.

2. Select a photo in a shared album so that it's displayed full screen, then swipe up to view when the photo was posted, along with comments from others.

3. To mark a photo as one you like, press the Touch surface.

Delete a shared album

1. Open the Photos app on Apple TV, then swipe to the Shared category in the menu bar.

Note: If you don't see the Shared category, go to Settings > Users and Accounts > iCloud and turn on Shared Albums.

2. Select an album from My Albums, then select People.

3. Select Delete Shared Stream.

The album is removed from Apple TV, but not from iCloud.

Create a   photo screen saver on Apple TV

You can use shared photos or albums in the Photos app as your Apple TV screen saver.

Set a screen saver

1. Open the Photos app on Apple TV, then swipe to the Shared category in the menu bar.

   Note: If you don't see the Shared category, go to Settings > Users and Accounts > iCloud and turn on Shared Albums.

2. Select an album, then select Set as Screen saver and confirm.

Adjust screen saver settings

1. Open Settings on Apple TV.

2. Go to General > Screen Saver.

Create a slideshow on Apple TV

You can view your shared photos and albums as a slideshow on Apple TV.

Create a slideshow and adjust slideshow settings

1. Open the Photos app on Apple TV, then swipe to the Shared category in the menu bar.

   Note: If you don't see the Shared category, go to Settings > Users and Accounts > iCloud and turn on Shared Albums.

2. Select an album or Photo Stream in My Albums, then select Play Slideshow.

3. Select to adjust any of the following settings:

   o *Shuffle Photos:* Turn on to show your photos in random order.

   o *Repeat Photos:* Turn on to play the slideshow continuously.

   o *Theme:* Select a slideshow theme to apply a different style to your slideshow.

   o *Time Per Slide:* Select how long to display each photo on the screen.

130

- *Transition:* Select the transition effect used between photos.

4. Select Start Slideshow.

Chapter 7

The App Store

Find apps in the Apple TV App Store

Use the App Store  o browse, purchase, and download apps to Apple TV.

Browse or search the App Store

1. Open the App Store on Apple TV.

2. In the menu bar, swipe to any of the following categories:

   ○ *Discover:* Browse a great selection of apps chosen   by the App Store.

   ○ *Apps:* Browse apps by category.

   ○ *Games:* Browse games in the App Store.

○ *Arcade:* Browse games available in Apple Arcade, an ad-free subscription-based gaming service.

○ *Purchased:* See the apps you've purchased in the App Store—including any apps purchased on other iOS or iPadOS devices that have a custom Apple TV version of the app, as well as purchases by Family Sharing members.

○ Q *Search:* Enter a search term to find apps by name.

Use Siri to find apps

You can use Siri to dictate while using Search or at any time to find apps on Apple TV.

Do one of the following:

- In the Search screen of the App Store, highlight the text entry field, press and hold the Siri button on the Siri Remote, and speak.

- From anywhere else on Apple TV, press and hold the Siri button on the Siri Remote, and speak.

You can search for apps by name, developer, or category.

Ask Siri. Say something like:

- o "Find Crossey Road"

- o "Find weather apps"

- o "What are some new sports apps?"

- o "Find apps by Apple"

Note: If you get movie and TV results instead of apps, try including "app" at the end of your Siri request: "Find Crossey Road app."

Access family members' apps

With Family Sharing enabled, you can view and download apps purchased by other family members.

- In the Purchased screen of the App Store 🅰️ on Apple TV, select Family Sharing, then select the name of a family member.

Purchase and download apps on Apple TV

Download an app

- In the App Store  on Apple TV, highlight Buy or Get (for a free app), then press the Touch surface of the Siri Remote to begin downloading.

  If you see Install (with the iCloud icon), you've already purchased the app and you can download it again for free. If you see Open, the app is already installed; select Open to launch the app.

While an app is downloading or updating, its icon appears on the Home screen with a progress indicator.

Tip: If you set up Family Sharing, your family organizer can review purchases made by other family members under the age of 18. For example, if Ask to Buy is set for younger family members   (configured in System Preferences on a Mac running   macOS Catalina, in iTunes on a Mac running macOS Mojave or earlier, or on an iOS or iPadOS device), then   when those members try to make a purchase, a message is sent to the family organizer asking for   approval.

Restrict in-app purchases

Many apps provide   extra content or enhancements for a fee. You can limit purchases that can be made within an app.

1. Open Settings on Apple TV.

2. Go   to   General   >   Restrictions   (make   sure Restrictions is turned on) and turn off In-App Purchases.

Set up automatic updates or installation

By default, apps   are automatically updated when new versions are released. You can turn this feature on or off.

You can also set   Apple TV to automatically add apps that have an Apple TV version whenever you download apps on an iPhone or iPad signed in to the same iTunes account.

1. Open Settings on Apple TV.

2. Go to Apps, then do either of the following:

   ○ *Turn automatic updates on or off:* Select Automatically Update apps.

     If Automatically Update Apps is turned off, you can select any app in the App Store to check if an update is available and manually update there.

   ○ *Turn automatic app installation on or off:* Select Automatically Install Apps.

Note: Family members' apps are not automatically added to the Home screen.

Chapter 8

Podcast

Get podcasts on Apple TV

Open the Apple Podcasts app  to access your favorite podcasts on Apple TV.

Find and play podcasts

1. Open the Podcasts app on Apple TV.

2. In the menu bar, swipe to any of the following categories:

   o *Listen Now:* Browse episodes you haven't heard or watched, or resume episodes you haven't finished yet.

   o *Library:* See a list of your podcasts and the stations you've created.

- Featured: Browse featured podcasts.

- Top Charts: Browse the most popular podcasts by genre.

- Search: Use the onscreen keyboard to enter a search term.

3. To preview or stream an episode, select the podcast, then select an episode.

Use Siri to find podcasts

Do one of the following:

- In the Search screen of the Podcast app 🎙️on Apple TV, highlight the text entry field, press and hold the Siri button 🎙️on the Siri Remote, then speak.

  For example, say the name of the podcast you're looking for.

- From anywhere else on Apple TV, press and hold the Siri button 🎙️on the Siri Remote and ask for a podcast by name, followed by the word "podcast."

Apple TV opens the Podcasts app and adds your request to its search screen. If you've already subscribed to the podcast, it begins playing the current episode.

Get new episodes as they're released

Subscribe to a podcast to get new episodes as they become available.

- While browsing in Featured or Top Charts in the Podcasts app on Apple TV, select a podcast, then select Subscribe.

Delete unplayed episodes

- In the Podcasts app on Apple TV, swipe to go to Listen Now, highlight an individual episode, press and hold the Touch surface, then select Delete.

Control podcast playback on Apple TV

Once a podcast starts playing, it appears in the Now Playing screen. The podcast continues to play even if you leave Podcasts, but it stops if you begin playing video or audio in another app.

On the Now Playing screen, you can control playback, navigate to other podcasts, or select more options.

Ask Siri. Say: "Play" or "Pause"

Control podcast playback

1. With the Now Playing screen open on Apple TV, rest your finger on the Touch surface of the Siri Remote.

   Podcasts or episodes adjacent to the current podcast appear in the Now Playing queue. A timeline also appears showing elapsed and remaining time. When the timeline is active, you can also press the Touch surface to play or pause the podcast.

2. Do any of the following:

   - *Pause or play:* Press the Play/Pause button ▶︎❙❙on the Siri Remote.

   - *Rewind or fast forward:* Press and hold the left or right side of the Touch surface to rewind or fast forward during playback. Release to resume playback.

   - *Go back to the beginning or skip to the next podcast or episode:* Press the left or right side of the Touch surface to restart the current podcast or episode or to skip to the start of the next podcast or episode.

- *Skip backward or forward 10 seconds:* Swipe down to highlight the play head. Press the left or right side of the Touch surface to skip backward or forward. Press again to skip another 10 seconds.

- *Play a different podcast:* Swipe left or right to highlight the podcast you want to play, then press the Touch surface.

- *Move to a specific point in the podcast or episode:* Swipe down to highlight the play head, then swipe left or right to move backward or forward on the timeline.

Change Airplay audio settings

1. With the Now Playing screen open on Apple TV, rest your finger on the Touch surface of the Siri Remote, then swipe up and select the more button ⚇at the top of the screen.

2. Swipe left and select the Airplay button 🛜to see more options.

See more options

- With the Now Playing screen open on Apple TV, rest your finger on the Touch surface of the Siri Remote, then swipe up to highlight the More button ⬤at the top of the screen to see more options:

  - Mark the podcast as played or unplayed

  - View a full description of the podcast

  - Subscribe to the podcast.

Organize podcasts into stations on Apple TV

You can organize your favorite podcasts to which you've subscribed into stations that update automatically across all of your devices.

Create a podcast station

1. Open the Podcasts app ⬤on Apple TV.

2. Swipe to go to Library, then select Create a Station

3. Enter a name for your station, then select done.

4. Add podcasts to your station by choosing from the list of subscribed podcasts. To create additional stations, select the New Station button ✛in Library.

Browse station episodes

1. Open the Podcasts app on Apple TV.

2. Swipe to go to Library, then select a station to see a list of episodes.

3. To play an episode, highlight it, then press the Touch surface or the Play/Pause button ▶❚❚of the Siri Remote.

Get more options from the episode list

1. Open the Podcasts app on Apple TV.

2. To see a list of episodes, swipe to go to Library, then select a station.

3. Highlight a podcast, then press and hold the Touch surface of the Siri Remote to see more options:

    o Play the next episode

    o Add the current episode to Up Next

    o Mark the episode as played

    o View a full description of the episode

    o Delete the episode

Get more options for a station

144

1. Open the Podcasts app on Apple TV.

2. Swipe to go to Library, then highlight a station.

3. Press and hold the Touch surface of the Siri Remote to see more options:

   o Play the station

   o Refresh the station to see the newest episodes

   o Go to that station's settings

   o Delete the station

Change a station's settings

1. Open the Podcasts app on Apple TV.

2. Swipe to go to Library, then select a station.

3. Select Station Settings, then select menu items to:

   o Rename the station

   o Change the playback order of episodes

   o Change which episodes, type of media, and playback status to include

   o Add or choose different subscribed podcasts for the station

145

o Delete the   station

Adjust podcast settings on Apple TV

Adjust settings for   Podcasts

1. Open Settings on Apple TV.

2. Go to Apps > Podcasts   to do any of the following:

   o *Allow Podcasts to refresh your subscriptions in the   background:* Turn on Background App Refresh.

   o *Sync   podcasts with your other iOS and iPadOS devices:* Turn on Sync Podcasts.

   o *Automatically   start playing   the   next episode after the current one ends:* Turn on Continuous   Playback.

   o *Set podcasts defaults:* Choose how often Podcasts checks your subscriptions for new episodes   and choose whether to keep episodes after you finish them.

   o *Use custom   colors based on the artwork for each podcast:* Turn on Custom Colors.

Show the screen saver while listening to podcasts

1. Open Settings on Apple TV.

2. Go to General > Screen Saver and turn on Show during Music and Podcasts.

Chapter 9

iTunes movies and TV shows

Watch iTunes movies and TV shows on Apple TV

With the iTunes Movies 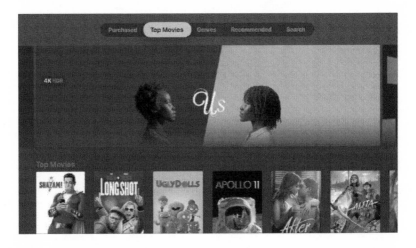 and TV Shows apps, the latest movies and hit TV shows are always available.

Tip: You can also access all iTunes movies and TV shows directly in the Apple TV app .

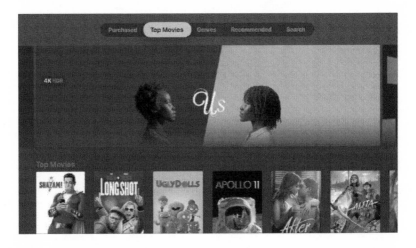

Find and watch iTunes movies and TV shows

1. Open iTunes Movies or TV Shows on Apple TV.

2. In the menu bar, swipe to any of the following categories:

○ *Purchased:* See the movies you've purchased on the iTunes Store, including purchases made on other iOS or iPadOS devices and purchases by Family Sharing members.

○ *Top Movies* or *Top TV Shows:* Browse the top items in the iTunes Store.

○ *Wish List/Favorites:* Find items you've added to your Wish List (Movies) or Favorites (TV shows) but haven't yet purchased or rented.

○ *Genres:* Browse by genre.

○ *Recommended:* Find recommendations based on your previous purchases.

○ *Search:* Enter a search term to find movies or TV shows.

3. Select an item to see ratings, descriptions, and purchase or rental information.

Get an extended description.

Select to rent.

Select to buy.

Watch a preview.

4. Do any of the   following:

   o *Watch a free preview:* Select Preview.

   o *Buy an   item:* Select Buy, then confirm that
     you want to buy it. For TV shows, you can
     buy   an   entire   season   or   individual
     episodes.

   o *Rent a movie:* In some regions, you can
     rent movies.   Select Rent, then confirm
     that you want to rent it.

     You have   30 days to begin watching a
     rented movie. After you start watching it,
     you can play it as many times as you want
     within 48 hours. During the rental period,
     you can download   the rented movie on

one device at any given time and also stream it on another. For example, you can start watching a movie downloaded on your iPhone, then finish watching it later on your Apple TV. Once your time is up, the movie is no longer available.

○ *Add an item to your wish list:* When you find something you might want to buy or rent later, select Wish List⊕. To view you're Wish List, swipe to Wish List in the menu bar.

○ *Remove an item from your wish list:* Swipe to Wish List in the menu bar, then select the item. Select Remove ⊖on the item's details page.

When you buy or rent a movie from the iTunes Store, it automatically plays in the highest-quality format available for your Apple TV, including high-definition (HD) and 4K resolution formats. These videos might also feature high dynamic range (HDR) in HDR10 or Dolby Vision, and Dolby Atmos.

Use Siri to find movies and TV shows

151

On Apple TV, do one of the   following:

- In the Search screen, highlight the text entry field, press and hold the   Siri button 🎤on the Siri Remote, and speak.

- From anywhere else on   Apple TV, press and hold the Siri button 🎤on the Siri Remote, and speak.

Access family members'   purchases

With Family Sharing turned on, you can view movies and TV shows purchased by   other family members.

- In iTunes movies [movies] or TV shows [tv shows] on Apple TV, swipe to   Purchase in the menu bar, choose Family Sharing, then select the name of a family member in the   list.

  Note: To set up Family   Sharing or change settings, you need to use a Mac or an iOS or iPadOS device such as iPhone   or iPad.

If Apple TV is using the iTunes account of an "Ask to Buy" user, the family organizer is sent   a message asking for approval before the purchase is completed. Age restrictions for "Ask to Buy" vary by   area. Using iTunes on a computer, family members can hide any of their purchases so other family members can't view them.

Change iTunes movie and TV show settings on Apple TV

Adjust settings for iTunes movies and TV shows

1. Open Settings on Apple TV.

2. Go to Apps > iTunes Movies and TV Shows and do any of the following:

   - *Change the video resolution for purchases and rentals:* By default, you rent, purchase, and play back iTunes videos in the highest resolution possible, which requires a fast Internet connection. If you have a slower connection, select Video Resolution and choose Good.

   - *Turn Quick Start on or off:* By default, videos will play instantly in the best resolution available. You can turn this off if your Internet connection is slower.

   Note: If Quick Start is turned off, 4K streaming and Dolby Atoms are disabled.

o *Limit Purchases and Rentals to SD:* If you have a slow Internet connection or want to use less data, turn this on to purchase and rent videos in standard definition.

o *Sort Movies in Wish List:* Choose either By Date to show recently added movies first, or alphabetically to show movies in alphabetical order.

o *Sort TV Shows in in Favorites:* Choose either By Date to show recently added TV shows first, or alphabetically to show TV shows in alphabetical order.

Search on Apple TV

Apple TV includes a Search app 🔍 that can help you locate movies, TV shows, cast and crew information, apps in the App Store 🅰, and even music if you're an Apple Music subscriber.

Search using the onscreen keyboard

1. Highlight the Search app 🔍 on the Home screen of Apple TV, then press the Touch surface of the Siri Remote.

2. Type your query using the onscreen keyboard.

The Search app returns content associated with your search terms.

Tip: You can use the keyboard on a nearby iPhone or iPad to enter text directly on Apple TV instead of using the Siri Remote.

Note: Apps included in search results may vary based on region.

Dictate instead of typing

You can also enter search terms in the Search app using voice dictation.

- Press and hold the Siri button 🎤on the Siri Remote, then speak.

Select a search result

- Select an item in the list of results to see additional details.

  Information about the item appears, including all of the apps where the content is available.

Chapter 10

Home Sharing

Stream content with Home Sharing on Apple TV

You can stream music, movies, TV shows, photos, and other content from a computer, an iOS device, or an iPadOS device to your Apple TV. Both the device and Apple TV must be signed in with the same Apple ID, and both must have Home Sharing turned on.

Set up Home Sharing on Apple TV

1. Open Settings on Apple TV, then Go to Users and Accounts > Home Sharing.

2. Turn on Home Sharing, then enter your Apple ID and password.

3. To configure your devices, do any of the following:

   ○ *Configure a Mac with macOS Catalina or later:* On your Mac, choose Apple menu □ > System Preferences, then click Sharing. Select the Media Sharing checkbox, then select the Home Sharing checkbox and enter your Apple ID and password.

- o *Configure a Mac with macOS Mojave and earlier, or a Windows PC:* In iTunes, go to File > Home Sharing and choose Turn on Home Sharing. Enter your Apple ID and password, then click Turn on Home Sharing.

  Note: In Windows 7 and Windows 8, iTunes menus are hidden by default. To show them temporarily, press and hold the Alt key.

- o *Configure an iOS or iPadOS device:* In Settings on the device, go to Music or TV > iTunes Videos. Turn on Home Sharing, then enter your Apple ID and password.

4. Once you've configured all of your devices with the same Apple ID, open the Computers app on the Apple TV Home screen.

Libraries from your shared devices appear, and you can view or play content from any library.

View photos from your Mac on Apple TV

With Home Sharing enabled, you can share photos from your computer on Apple TV. Select which photos you want to share based on albums in Photos on a Mac, or just choose a folder on your Mac.

Share photos to Apple TV (macOS Catalina or later)

1. On your Mac, choose Apple menu □ > System Preferences, then click Sharing.

2. Make sure Home Sharing and Media Sharing are selected, then enter the Apple ID and password used to create your Home Share.

3. Select "Share photos with Apple TV," then click Choose.

4. Click the "Share Photos from" pop-up menu and make sure your preferred photos app has a checkmark, then choose a folder to share.

5. Choose whether you want to share all your photos and albums or just selected albums, then click OK.

   The photo albums or folders you share appear in the Computers app on Apple TV.

Share photos to Apple TV (macOS Mojave or earlier)

1. In iTunes on your Mac, go to File > Home Sharing > Choose Photos to Share with Apple TV.

   The Photo Sharing Preferences window opens.

2. Select "Share Photos from," then select Photos or iPhoto, or choose a folder to share.

3. Choose whether you want to share photos and albums or just selected albums, then click Apply.

   The photo albums or folders you share appear in the Computers app on Apple TV.

Chapter 11

Beyond Basics

Restrict access to content on Apple TV

You can configure Apple TV to restrict certain content so only authorized users can watch, download or play items from search results, or make purchases. This is often also referred to as *parental controls*. You can restrict a variety of content and activities, such as:

- Purchasing movies, TV shows, and apps

- Making in-app purchases

- Playing iTunes movies or TV shows based on content ratings

- Opening apps based on age ratings

- Playing content identified as explicit

- Blocking downloads or playback of items from search results for content identified as explicit

- Playing multiplayer games in Game Center

- Adding friends in Game Center

- Changing Airplay or Location settings

Note: Restrictions may not apply to third-party apps. To restrict third-party content, adjust the settings for the individual apps either inside the apps, or in the Apps area of Settings ⚙.

To set or override restrictions, you must enter the passcode.

Turn on restrictions

1. Open Settings ⚙ on Apple TV.

2. Go to   General > Restrictions, turn on restrictions, and enter a 4-digit passcode.

   Once you enter and verify the passcode, restrictions and other options in the Restrictions menu are enabled.

Change the passcode

1. Open Settings ⚙ on Apple TV.

2. Go to General > Restrictions.

3. Select   Change Passcode, enter the current passcode, and then enter the new passcode.

Configure what types of content are restricted

1. Open Settings ⚙ on Apple TV.

2. Go to   General > Restrictions, and enter the passcode if required.

3. Select   options to restrict iTunes Store purchases and rentals, allowed content types, Game Center settings, and   other settings.

You must first turn on restrictions to configure the Restrictions   settings. To access restricted content, you must enter the passcode each time.

Remove all restrictions

You can temporarily   remove all restrictions and then add them back again later.

1. Open Settings on Apple TV.

2. Go to General   > Restrictions, then select Restrictions.

3. Enter the   passcode, then set Restrictions to Off.

If you use Family Sharing, you can also use your iOS or iPadOS device to   limit the content your family members can buy—including enabling Ask to buy, which lets your kids   purchase items only with parental approval.

Manage Apple TV storage

Your Apple TV   streams video and music, but it stores apps locally. The more apps you download to Apple TV, the more storage   is used up. At some point you may get a warning that you're running out of disk space. If so, you can remove   apps to free up space.

Check the Apple TV storage levels

1. Open Settings 🔘 on Apple TV.

2. Go to   General > Manage Storage.

   A list of the apps on your Apple TV shows how much   space each item is using.

Delete apps to recover space

1. Open   Settings 🔘 on Apple TV.

2. Go to General > Manage Storage.

3. Highlight   the trash icon for any item in the list and press the Touch surface.

   The app   and all of its data are removed from the device.

   You can   also delete apps directly on the Home screen.

   If you   delete an app, you can download it again from the App Store without repurchasing it.

Share Apple TV with multiple users

It's easy to share Apple TV with multiple family members. When each member in a household has an Apple ID, switching member profiles on Apple TV creates a custom experience, with Up Next lists, music, and content recommendations personalized for the currently active user.

Note: Changing users does not change the Apple ID used for iCloud. To change your iCloud account, open Settings on Apple TV and go to Users and Accounts > iCloud.

Switch the account used to purchase movies, TV shows, and apps

On Apple TV, do either of the following:

- Open Settings , go to Users and Accounts > Current User, then select a name from the list and sign in to that account.

- Open tvOS Control Center, then select the name of a different family member. Only one user at a time can be active on the Apple TV.

Change an iCloud account

1. Open Settings on Apple TV.

2. Go to Users and Accounts > iCloud > Sign Out, then select Sign In and enter a new Apple ID.

Change a Game Center account

1. Open Settings on Apple TV.

2. Go to Users and Accounts > Game Center > Sign Out, then select Sign In and enter a new Apple ID.

Family Sharing on Apple TV

Family Sharing lets you share apps and viewing privileges with up to six family members. One adult in your household—the family organizer—invites family members to join the family group and agrees to pay for any iTunes Store or App Store purchases made by family members. (Family sharing, which works across all your Apple devices, is different from multiuser switching on Apple TV.)

Important: You can't initiate or configure Family Sharing directly on Apple TV. It must be done on a Mac, an iOS device, or an iPadOS device.

Adjust video and audio settings on Apple TV

On Apple TV, you can customize your viewing and listening experience. For example, you can:

- Make sure the Apple TV output resolution matches your television's native resolution

- Control whether Apple TV switches frame rate and dynamic range settings to match the video content

- Control whether Apple TV outputs Dolby Digital encoded audio

- Send audio output to Bluetooth® headphones or alternative speakers

- Decide what language to use for subtitles and audio tracks in foreign language content

Watch Apple TV without disturbing others

Apple TV can lower the overall sound level by reducing the loudness of music and sound effects.

Do either of the following:

- *Reduce loudness in the currently playing video:* Swipe down to show the Info pane, select Audio, then select Reduce Loud Sounds.

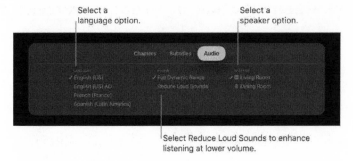

Select a
language option.

Select a
speaker option.

Select Reduce Loud Sounds to enhance
listening at lower volume.

- *Reduce loudness for all videos:* Open Settings on Apple TV, go to Video and Audio, and turn on Reduce Loud Sounds.

Set the language of audio and subtitles

1. Open Settings on Apple TV.

2. Go to Video and Audio and select the language you want under Audio Language or Subtitle Language.

   Note: If the language you select isn't available, the default language is used—it's the one associated with your region, or the one that's selected in General Settings.

Send audio to Air Pods, Bluetooth headphones, or another Airplay speaker

1. Open Settings on Apple TV.

2. Go to Video and Audio, select Audio Output, and
   then select an option.

Adjust other audio and video settings

You can adjust other audio or video settings, such as
Sound Effects and Music, Navigation Clicks, Audio
Format, HDMI Output, and Resolution.

1. Open Settings on Apple TV.

2. Go to Video and Audio.

3. Change any of the following:

   ○ *Video output format:* Select Format, then
      choose the resolution, frame rate, and
      dynamic range settings for video playback.

   ○ *Audio format:* By default, Apple TV uses the
      best audio format available. You can
      change the audio format if you're
      experiencing problems with playback.
      Select Audio Format, then select Change
      Format and choose either Dolby Atoms,
      Dolby Digital 5.1, or Stereo.

   ○ *Dynamic range matching:* Apple TV can
      automatically switch the dynamic range

setting during playback to match the dynamic range of the video content. Select Match Content, then turn on Match Dynamic Range.

o *Frame rate matching:* Apple TV can automatically switch the frame rate and dynamic range during playback to match the frame rate and dynamic range of the video content. Select Match Content, then turn on Match Dynamic Range and Match Frame Rate.

Set the Home button destination on Apple TV

Pressing the Home button once on your Siri Remote takes you to Up Next in the Apple TV App, and pressing the Home button again takes you to the Home screen.

You can change this setting so that pressing the Home button once takes you directly to the Home screen.

Change the Home button setting

1. Open Settings 	on Apple TV.

2. Go to Remotes and Devices, select Home Button, then select either Home Screen or Apple TV App.

Connect Bluetooth   devices to Apple TV

You may want to connect a Bluetooth® device to your Apple TV—such as an MFi-certified (made for iPhone, iPod touch, and iPad) game controller, a Sony PlayStation–compatible controller, a Microsoft Xbox One–compatible controller, Bluetooth headphones, a wireless keyboard, or another accessory.

Apple Air Pods connect automatically to Apple TV if they're associated with the same Apple ID.

Find and connect to a   nearby Bluetooth device

Before you start, refer to the device's instructions to set the device to Discoverable.

1. Open Settings on Apple TV, then go to Remotes and Devices >   Bluetooth.

2. Select the device in the list.

Use the iOS or iPadOS keyboard to enter text on Apple   TV

If you prefer not to enter text using the Siri Remote, you can set up a nearby iOS or iPadOS device to share its keyboard whenever a text field appears on Apple TV.

The iOS or iPadOS device must meet   certain minimum requirements.

Set up an iPhone or iPad to enter   text on Apple TV

- Make sure the iOS or iPadOS   device and Apple TV are both signed in to using the same Apple ID, and that Bluetooth® and Wi-Fi are   enabled on the iOS or iPadOS device.

Use an iOS or iPadOS keyboard   to type on Apple TV

Whenever a text field appears on   Apple TV, a notification appears on your iPhone or iPad.

- Tap the notification and enter text   in the iOS or iPadOS keyboard that appears.

  Text you enter on the iOS or   iPadOS device automatically appears in the text field on Apple TV.

Turn off the Apple TV keyboard on iOS or iPadOS

If you don't want your iOS or iPadOS   device to be used as a keyboard for Apple TV, turn off keyboard notifications on your iOS or iPadOS   device.

- On your iOS or iPadOS device, go to Settings > Notifications > Apple TV Keyboard and turn off Allow Notifications.

Control your TV and volume with the Siri Remote

You can configure the Siri Remote to turn your TV on or off, change the input to your Apple TV, and even control the volume.

Use the Siri Remote to turn your TV on or off

1. Open Settings on Apple TV.

2. Go to Remotes and Devices and turn on Turn on Your TV with Your Remote.

Use the Siri Remote to control the volume of your TV or receiver

1. Open Settings on Apple TV.

2. Go to Remotes and Devices > Volume Control and choose Auto.

Use other remotes to control Apple TV

You can use a network-based remote for home-control systems, or an infrared remote (commonly known as a *universal remote*) to control Apple TV.

A network-based remote sends signals to Apple TV through a network so the remote doesn't have to be pointed directly at Apple TV.

To use an infrared remote, you need to let it learn the signals that the Siri Remote generates.

Use a network-based remote with Apple TV

Before you can use a network-based remote for home-control systems with Apple TV, you first need to add the remote to the Home app on an iOS or iPadOS device. Make sure the remote is turned on and connected to your network.

1. Open the Home app on the iOS or iPadOS device.

2. Tap the Add button, tap Add Accessory, and then follow the onscreen instructions.

   You may need to scan or enter an 8-digit Home Kit setup code found on the remote itself (or on its box or in its documentation). You can assign the remote to a room, as well as give it a name. The name defines how it's shown in the Home app and on Apple TV, and also how you control it using Siri.

Teach an infrared remote to control Apple TV

1. Open Settings on Apple TV.

2. Go to Remotes and Devices > Learn Remote, then follow the onscreen instructions.

Stream to a conference room display

You can use Apple TV as a conference room display so that anyone can easily share their screen from a Mac, iOS device, or iPadOS device using AirPlay. When Conference Room Display is turned on, a message appears on the display with AirPlay connection instructions and wireless network details.

Turn on Conference Room Display

1. Open Settings on Apple TV.

2. Go to Airplay > Conference Room Display, then make sure Conference Room Display is turned on.

Create a custom message

1. Open Settings on Apple TV.

2. Go to Airplay > Conference Room Display > Custom Message, then enter your message.

Conference Room Display must be turned on to enter a message, and your message appears only when Apple TV is in Conference Room Display mode.

Choose a background

1. Open Settings on Apple TV.

2. Go to Airplay > Conference Room Display > Select Photo, then choose one of the photo-based background types.

   If you choose My Photos, the Photos app opens.

Preview Conference Room Display mode

1. Open Settings on Apple TV.

2. Go to Airplay > Conference Room Display, then go to Conference Room Display > Preview.

Lock Conference Room Display mode

You can set Apple TV so that Conference Room Display mode is locked until a 4-digit passcode is entered.

1. Open Settings on Apple TV.

2. Go to General > Restrictions, and enter the passcode if required.

3. Make sure Conference Room Display is set to restrictin the list of restricted items.

Note: You use the same 4-digit passcode you set in Restrictions to unlock Conference Room Display mode. If you forget the passcode, disconnect Apple TV from the power outlet, reconnect it, then press and hold the MENUbutton as it restarts. This temporarily unlocks Conference Room Display mode.

Change network settings on Apple TV

If you initially set up Apple TV using a wired network, you can change to a wireless network without having to set up Apple TV again.

1. Disconnect the Ethernet cable from Apple TV.

2. Open Settings ⚙ on Apple TV.

3. Select Network and join a Wi-Fi network.

Change the language or region format on Apple TV

The first time you set up Apple TV, you choose which display language and region format to use. You can change this later in Settings.

Change the language

1. Open Settings on Apple TV.

2. Go to General > Apple TV Language and select a language.

   Note: Siri and dictation may or may not be available, depending on the language you select.

Change the region format

1. Open Settings on Apple TV.

2. Go to General > Region and select a region.

Chapter 12

Restart, Reset, Update

Restart Apple TV

If Apple TV isn't responding, try restarting it.

Restart Apple TV

Do any of the following:

- Press and hold the MENU and Home ⬜buttons on the Siri Remote until the Apple TV status light blinks rapidly.

- Disconnect Apple TV from the power outlet, wait five seconds, then reconnect it.

- Open Settings ⚙ on Apple TV, go to System and select Restart.

Reset Apple TV

If you're having problems and Apple TV still doesn't respond after restarting, try resetting Apple TV to its factory settings. When you reset Apple TV, all data is erased, including your accounts and configuration.

You can also reset your Apple TV and update its software at the same time.

Reset Apple TV

1. Open Settings on Apple TV.

2. Go to System > Reset, then   select Reset.

Resetting Apple TV and restoring it to factory settings can take some   time, so be patient. If Apple TV still doesn't respond, do one of the following:

- o *If you have an Apple TV 4K:*Contact Apple TV Support.

- o *If you have an Apple TV HD and a PC with iTunes or   a Mac with macOS Mojave or earlier:* Disconnect the power and HDMI cables from   Apple TV. Connect one end of a USB-C cable (sold separately) to Apple TV and the other   end to your computer. Open iTunes on your computer, select Apple TV in the Source   list, then select restore. If that doesn't work, contact Apple TV Support.

- o *If you have an   Apple TV HD and a Mac with macOS Catalina or later:* Disconnect the power and   HDMI cables from Apple TV. Connect one end of a USB-C cable (sold separately) to   Apple TV and the other end to your computer. Open the Finder on your computer, select Apple TV in the sidebar, then select Restore. If that doesn't work, contact Apple TV Support.

Reset Apple TV and update software

1. Open Settings on Apple TV.

2. Go to System > Reset, then select Reset and Update.

Selecting this option restores your Apple TV to factory settings, erases all settings and information, and updates to the latest tvOS version.

Update Apple TV software

You'll see a message on Apple TV when a software update is available. You can also check for updates, or set Apple TV to update automatically.

Check for updates

1. Open Settings on Apple TV.

2. Go to System > Software Updates and select Update Software.

If an update is available, a message appears.

3. Select   Download   and   Install   to   start downloading.

During the update process, don't disconnect your Apple TV. The status   light may flash slowly during the update process.

Set automatic updates

1. Open Settings on Apple TV.

2. Go to System > Software   Updates and select Automatically Update.

Chapter 13

Accessibility

Accessibility features on Apple TV

Apple TV includes built-in accessibility features:

- *Siri:* The Siri Remote lets you use your voice to bypass onscreen navigation. Ask Siri to perform a wide range of tasks, such as "Find kid movies," "Rewind five minutes," "Open Music," and more. When the onscreen keyboard appears, highlight the text entry field and press and hold the Siri button 🎤. Dictate text or spell out user names and passwords instead of typing.

- *Closed Caption and SDH support:* Apple TV supports closed captioning, so those who are deaf or hard of hearing can fully enjoy new TV episodes and thousands of movies. Just look for the CC or SDH icon when you're browsing movies or TV shows on the iTunes Store. You can even customize captions with special styles and fonts.

- *Audio Descriptions:* Audio descriptions provide an explanation of important onscreen action and content in movies and TV shows. *Voiceover:*

Apple TV supports Voiceover, Apple's screen reader. Available in all the languages supported by Apple TV, and with support for Braille displays, Voiceover tells you exactly what's on your TV screen and helps you choose commands.

- *Zoom:* Zoom is a built-in magnifier that works anywhere on the Apple TV screen. With magnification adjustable up to 15 times the normal size, Zoom can help with a range of vision challenges.

- *Display Accommodations:* Change parameters on Apple TV for color differentiation, light sensitivity, and brightness. *Bold Text:* Choose Bold Text to make the text easier to read throughout the Apple TV interface.

- *Increase Contrast:* Increase contrast on the screen by reducing the transparency of background elements on Movie and TV Show pages, menu tabs, and more. You can also use a high-contrast cursor to better delineate the focused content. *Reduce Motion:* With Reduce Motion, some screen actions—such as moving between app icons on the Home screen and launching apps—are visually simpler.

- *Switch Control:* Control Apple TV using a connected Bluetooth® device or other platform as a switch.

Use subtitles and captioning on Apple TV

If you prefer special accessible captions, such as subtitles for the deaf and hard of hearing (SDH), you can set Apple TV to show them instead of standard subtitles and captions. You can also customize the look of subtitles and captions.

Note: Not all videos include closed captions.

Turn on Closed   Captions and SDH

1. In Settings on Apple TV, go to General >Accessibility > Subtitles and Captioning.

2. Turn Closed Captions and SDH on (or use the accessibility shortcut).

Turn closed captions on or off during video playback

- Press the Touch surface on the Siri Remote three times.

Note: When   Voiceover is turned on, this action instead turns audio descriptions on or off

Customize your subtitles and captions

1. In Settings   on Apple TV, go to General > Accessibility > Subtitles and Captioning > Style.

2. Choose an   existing caption style, or create a new style based on your choice of:

   o Font, size, and   color

   o Background color and opacity

   o Text opacity, edge   style, and highlight

Note: If you connect a Braille display to Apple TV, it will continuously print captions and   subtitles of a TV show or movie when captions or subtitles are turned on.

Use audio descriptions   on Apple TV

Audio descriptions provide an audible narration of important onscreen action and   content in movies and TV shows. If you have a video that includes audio descriptions, Apple TV can play   them for you.

Turn on audio descriptions

- In Settings 🔘 on Apple TV, go to General > Accessibility > Audio Descriptions (or use the accessibility shortcut).

Turn audio descriptions on or off during video playback

- When Voiceover is turned on, press the Touch surface on the Siri Remote three times.

  Note: When Voiceover is turned off, this action instead turns closed captions on or off.

Use Voiceover on Apple TV

Voiceover lets you control Apple TV without seeing the screen. You use simple gestures on the Touch surface of the Siri Remote to move around the screen, and listen as Voiceover speaks each item you highlight.

When you highlight an item, Voiceover first speaks the item and any associated text. After a short delay, Voiceover speaks any remaining text items on the screen, such as movie descriptions or actor listings.

Turn Voiceover on or off

- In Settings 🔘 on Apple TV, go to General > Accessibility > Voiceover (or use the accessibility shortcut).

Ask Siri. Say   something like:

- o "Turn Voiceover on"

- o "Turn   Voiceover off"

Operate the Voiceover rotor

The Voiceover rotor   is a touch control that lets you choose options by rotating two fingers on the Touch surface of the Siri   Remote.

- Rotate two fingers around a point on the Touch surface of the   Siri Remote to open the Voiceover rotor, which contains additional controls. The available rotor   controls vary, depending on what you're doing.

Explore Voiceover

As you drag your finger over the Touch surface on the Siri Remote, Voiceover   speaks each menu or text item you select.

1. To move your   selection, swipe up, down, left, or right.

2. To select the   previous or next rotor control, rotate two fingers left or right.

3. To adjust a rotor   control, swipe up or down.

188

For example, to adjust speech rate, rotate two fingers until the Voiceover speech rate rotor control is selected. Then swipe up or down to increase or decrease the speech rate.

4. To speak from the current text item to the bottom of the screen, swipe down with two fingers.

5. To speak the items on screen, starting at the top, swipe up with two fingers, or press and hold the Play button.

6. To pause speaking, tap once with two fingers. Tap again with two fingers to resume, or select another item.

Perform a custom rotor action with Voiceover

1. Rotate two fingers until Custom Actions is selected in the rotor.

2. Swipe up or down to hear each custom action, then press the Touch surface of the Siri Remote to perform an action.

Use a Bluetooth keyboard with VoiceOver on Apple TV

You can control VoiceOver with a connected Bluetooth® keyboard.

Use VoiceOver keyboard commands

Enter VoiceOver commands by pressing and holding the Control and Option keys together, then pressing one or more other keys. The Control-Option key combination is known as the *Voiceover key*, *VO* for short.

Type any of the following keyboard commands:

- *Turn on Voiceover Help:* VO-K

- *Turn off Voiceover Help:* Escape

- *Select the next or previous item:* VO-Right Arrow or VO-Left Arrow

- *Double-tap to activate the selected item:* VO-Space bar

- *Press the Home button:* VO-H

- *Touch and hold the selected item:* VO-Shift-M

- *Move to the status bar:* VO-M

- *Read from the current position:* VO-A

- *Read from the top:* VO-B

- *Pause or resume reading:* Control

- *Copy the last spoken text to the clipboard:* VO-Shift-C

- *Search for text:* VO-F

- *Mute or unmute Voiceover:* VO-S

- *Open the notifications screen:* Fn-VO-Up Arrow

- *Open Control Center:* Fn-VO-Down Arrow

- *Open the Item Chooser:* VO-I

- *Change the label of the selected item:* VO-/

- *Double-tap with two fingers:* VO-"-"

- *Swipe up or down:* VO-Up Arrow or VO-Down Arrow

- *Adjust the rotor:* VO-Command-Left Arrow or VO-Command-Right Arrow

- *Adjust the setting specified by the rotor:* VO-Command-Up Arrow or VO-Command-Down Arrow

- *Turn the screen curtain on or off:* VO-Shift-S

- *Return to the previous screen:* Escape

- *Switch apps:* Command-Tab or Command-Shift-Tab

Edit text using Voiceover

- Type the following commands to work with text (Voiceover reads the text as you move the insertion point):

  - *Go forward or back one character:* Right Arrow or Left Arrow

  - *Go forward or back one word:* Option-Right Arrow or Option-Left Arrow

  - *Go up or down one line:* Up Arrow or Down Arrow

  - *Go to the beginning or end of the line:* Command-Left Arrow or Command-Down Arrow

  - *Go to the beginning or end of the paragraph:* Option-Up Arrow or Option-Down Arrow

  - *Go to the previous or next paragraph:* Option-Up Arrow or Option-Down Arrow

- Go to the top or bottom of the text field: Command-Up Arrow or Command-Down Arrow

- Select text as you move: Shift + any of the insertion point movement commands above

- Select all text: Command-A

- Copy, cut, or paste the selected text: Command-C, Command-X, or Command-V

- Undo or redo last change: Command-Z or Shift-Command-Z

Use a braille display with Apple TV

You can use a Bluetooth® braille display to read VoiceOver output, and a braille display with input keys and other controls to control Apple TV when VoiceOver is turned on.

Connect a braille display

1. In Settings on Apple TV, go to General > Accessibility > VoiceOver > Braille.

2. Select Braille Display to pair the display with Apple TV.

When VoiceOver is used with a braille display, the display prints onscreen text for the item you are hovering over. As you move focus, VoiceOver speaks and the braille display prints the text. The braille display may include additional buttons that support basic Apple TV navigation.

Adjust braille settings

- In Settings 🔘 on Apple TV, go to General > Accessibility > VoiceOver > Braille, then do any of the following:

  - Select Output or Input, then select Contracted, Uncontracted Eight-dot, or Uncontracted Six-dot.

  - Select Automatic Translation, then select on or off.

  - Select Braille Tables, then select a table or choose Add Braille Table.

  - Select Alert Display Duration, then swipe to select a new duration.

Output closed captions in Braille during media playback

- In Settings ⚙ on Apple TV, go to General > Accessibility > Verbosity > Media Descriptions, then choose Braille or Speech and Braille.

Set the language for VoiceOver

- In Settings ⚙ on Apple TV, go to General > Language & Region, then choose a language option and region option.

  If you change the language for Apple TV, you may need to reset the language for VoiceOver and your braille display.

See an expanded description of the status cell

- On your braille display, press the status cell's router button.

Use Zoom to magnify the image on Apple TV

Use the Touch surface on the remote to control Zoom and to pan around the zoomed image.

Turn Zoom on or off

- In Settings ⚙ on Apple TV, go to General > Accessibility > Zoom and turn Zoom on.

  You can also set up an accessibility shortcut to activate Zoom.

Zoom in or out

- With Zoom turned on, press the Touch surface of the Siri Remote three times.

  Any item you highlight is automatically magnified.

Move the zoom focus

- Tap the top, bottom, left, or right edge of the Touch surface of the Siri Remote to move in that direction by one screen item.

Adjust the magnification

- Tap the Touch surface of the Siri Remote and drag up or down with two fingers.

  To limit the maximum magnification, in Settings on Apple TV go to General > Accessibility > Zoom > Maximum Zoom Level.

Turn panning on or off

- Tap the Touch surface of the Siri Remote with two fingers.

Pan to see more

- While panning, drag your finger on the Touch surface of the Siri Remote.

Speak the currently selected screen item

- Press the Siri button 🎤twice.

Use Display Accommodations on Apple TV

You can change parameters on Apple TV for color differentiation, light sensitivity, and brightness.

Tip: To invert light and dark colors on Apple TV, turn on Dark mode.

Turn on Color Filters

This setting is for users who are color blind or have difficulty reading text on the display.

- In Settings 🔘on Apple TV, go to General > Accessibility > Display Accommodations, then turn on Color Filters.

  You can select from a variety of filters used to differentiate colors.

Turn on Light Sensitivity

This setting adjusts the level of dimness or brightness on your display.

1. In Settings 🔘on Apple TV, go to General > Accessibility > Display Accommodations, then turn on Light Sensitivity.

2. Select Intensity, then swipe to adjust the percentage of display intensity.

Turn on Reduce White Point

This setting adjusts the brightness level of colors on your display.

1. In Settings on Apple TV, go to General > Accessibility > Display Accommodations, then turn on Reduce White Point.

2. Select Intensity, then swipe to adjust the percentage of white point intensity.

Display bold text   on Apple TV

You can make text on Apple TV easier to read by displaying onscreen text with boldface type.

Turn on bold text

- In Settings on Apple TV, go to General >Accessibility, then turn on Bold Text.

Increase Apple TV   screen contrast

There are two ways you can increase the screen contrast to make items easier to see   on Apple TV.

Remove blurred image backgrounds

- In Settings ⚙ on Apple TV, go to General >
Accessibility > Increase Contrast, then turn on
Reduce Transparency.

Highlight selected items further

- In Settings ⚙ on Apple TV, go to General >
Accessibility > Increase Contrast > Focus Style,
then choose High Contrast.

Reduce screen motion on Apple TV

You can stop the movement of app icons, movie
posters, and some other screen elements on Apple TV.

Reduce motion

- In Settings ⚙ on Apple TV, go to General >
Accessibility >Motion, then do any of the
following:

  - *Reduce the amount of motion displayed by
Apple TV during navigation:* Turn on Reduce
Motion.

  - *Turn off automatic playback of video
previews:* Turn off Auto-Play Video
Previews.

About Switch   Control on Apple TV

Switch Control is an assistive technology that lets you control Apple TV by   clicking a keyboard key, mouse button, or other control on a Bluetooth®-connected device as a switch. Use   any of several methods to perform actions such as   selecting, dragging, and typing. You use a switch to select   an item on the screen, and then use the same (or different) switch to choose an action to perform on that   item or location. The basic methods are:

- *Item   scanning   (default),*   which   highlights different items on the screen until you select one

- *Manual selection,* which lets you move   from item to item on demand (requires multiple switches)

Whichever method you use, when you   select an individual item (rather than a group), a menu appears so you can choose how to act on the   selected item (press or drag).

If you use multiple switches, you can set   up each switch to perform a specific action and customize your item selection method. For   example, instead of automatically scanning screen items, you can set up switches to move to the next or previous item on demand.

You can adjust the behavior of Switch Control in a variety of ways, to suit your specific needs and style.

Turn on Switch Control on Apple TV

To connect a switch to Apple TV, you can connect an external Bluetooth® device such as a keyboard, or you can use the platform-switching feature that forwards switch actions from another device such as an iPhone or a Mac. On an iOS or iPadOS device, tap the screen to trigger the switch. (On iPhone 6s and iPhone 6s Plus or later, force-click the screen.)

Add a switch and choose its action

- In Settings on Apple TV, go to General > Accessibility > Switch Control > Switches, select Add New Switch, then follow the onscreen instructions.

   If you add only one switch, it functions as the Select Item switch by default.

   If you're adding an external switch, you need to connect it to Apple TV before it will appear in the list of available switches. Follow the instructions that came with the switch. If the switch connects using Bluetooth, you need to pair the device with Apple TV.

Turn Switch Control on or off

- In Settings ⚙ on Apple TV, go to General > Accessibility, then turn Switch Control on or off.

Use Switch Control on Apple TV

Here are some basic techniques for using Switch Control.

Select an item

- While the item is highlighted on Apple TV, trigger the switch you've set up as your Select Item switch.

  If you're using a single switch, it functions as the Select Item switch by default.

Perform an action on the selected item

Choose a command from the control menu that appears when you select the item. The layout of the menu depends on how you configure press behavior.

- In Settings ⚙ on Apple TV, go to General > Accessibility > Switch Control > Press Behavior and choose an option:

  - *With Default on:* The control menu usually includes only the Press button and the More button (two dots at the bottom). If you're in a scrollable area of the screen, a scroll bar also appears. To press the highlighted item, trigger your Select Item button when Press is highlighted. To see additional action buttons, choose more at the bottom of the menu. If you have multiple switches, you can set one up specifically for pressing.

  - *With Auto Press on:* To press the item, do nothing—the item is automatically tapped when the Auto Press interval expires (0.75 seconds if you haven't changed it). To see the control menu, trigger your Select Item button before the Auto Press interval expires. The control menu skips the Press button and goes right to the full set of action buttons.

o *With Always Press on:* Press to select the highlighted item rather than display the control menu. Wait until the end of the scan cycle, then press a button to display the control menu.

Scroll the screen

- Select an item in a scrollable part of the screen on Apple TV:

  o *With Auto Press off:* Choose the Scroll Down button (next to the Press button) in the control menu. Or, for more scrolling options, choose More, then choose Scroll.

  o *With Auto Press on:* Choose Scroll from the control menu. If many actions are available, you might have to choose more first.

  o *Press the Home button.* Choose Home from the control menu.

Control media playback

- On Apple TV, choose Media Controls from the Scanner menu to play, pause, or go backward or forward.

Dismiss the control menu without choosing an action

On Apple TV, do one of the following:

- Press while the original item is highlighted and all the icons in the control menu are dimmed.

- Choose Escape from the control menu.

  The menu goes away after cycling the number of times you specify in Settings ⚙, at General > Accessibility > Switch Control > Loops.

Perform other hardware actions

- On Apple TV, select any item, choose Device from the menu that appears, then use the menu to mimic these actions:

  - Click the multitasking menu button for multitasking

  - Press the volume buttons

  - Triple-click the Menu button

Use Switch Control item scanning on Apple TV

Item scanning alternately highlights each item or group of items on the entire screen until you trigger your Select Item switch. If there are many items,

Switch Control highlights them in groups. When you select a group, highlighting continues with the items in the group. When you select a unique item, scanning stops and the control menu appears. Item scanning is the default when you first turn on Switch Control.

You can choose from three scanning styles:

- *Auto scanning* automatically highlights items, one after the other.

- *Manual scanning* uses one switch to highlight an item and another to activate it.

- *Single-switch step scanning* uses a switch to move the highlight from item to item. If you take no action after a period of time, the highlighted item activates.

Select an item or enter a group

1. Watch (or listen) as items are highlighted.

2. When the item you want to control (or the group containing the item) is highlighted, trigger your Select Item switch.

3. Work your way down the hierarchy of items until you select the individual item you want to control.

Back out of a group

- Trigger your Select Item switch when the dashed highlight around the group or item appears.

Dismiss the control menu without performing an action

Do one of the following:

- Trigger your Select Item switch when the item itself is highlighted.

- Choose Escape from the control menu.

Hear the names of items as they're highlighted

Do one of the following:

- In Settings on Apple TV, go to General > Accessibility > Switch Control, then turn on Speech.

- Choose Settings from the control menu, then choose Speech On.

Slow down or speed up the scanning

8

- In Settings on Apple TV, go to General > Accessibility > Switch Control > Auto Scanning Time.

Adjust basic Switch Control settings

- In Settings on Apple TV, go to General > Accessibility > Switch Control, where you can:

  - Add switches and specify their function

  - Adjust how rapidly items are scanned

  - Turn off auto scanning (only if you've added a Move to Next Item switch)

  - Set scanning to pause on the first item in a group

  - Choose how many times to cycle through the screen before hiding Switch Control

  - Set whether a movement action is repeated when you hold down a switch, and how long to wait before repeating

  - Add another action to a switch by holding down the switch for a long duration

- Choose a Press behavior and set the interval for performing a second switch action to show the control menu

- Set whether and how long you need to hold a switch down before it's accepted as a switch action

- Have Switch Control ignore accidental repeated switch triggers

- Turn on sound effects or have items read aloud as they're scanned

- Choose which items appear in menus and the order in which they appear

- Choose what to include in the Switch Control menu

- Set whether items should be grouped while item scanning

- Make the selection cursor larger or a different color

Fine-tune Switch Control settings

- Choose Settings from the control menu to:

  - Adjust scanning speed

o Change the   location of the control menu

o Turn sound or speech accompaniment on or off

o Turn off groups to scan items one at a time

o Change   the cursor color.

Set hearing controls on Apple TV

You can set hearing   controls so that Apple TV outputs only mono audio. You can also adjust the balance of audio between left and   right speakers.

Turn on mono audio

- In Settings ⊚on Apple TV, go to General > Accessibility, then turn on Mono Audio.

Adjust audio balance

- In Settings ⊚on Apple TV, go to General > Accessibility, then   select Balance and adjust the slide control.

Add an accessibility   shortcut to Apple TV

You can add an accessibility shortcut to the MENU button on the Siri Remote. When   you press the MENU button three times, the shortcut launches.

Add an accessibility   shortcut

- In Settings 🔘 on Apple TV, go to General > Accessibility > Accessibility Shortcut and select an option.

Use your accessibility shortcut

- On the Siri Remote, press the MENU button three times.

Chapter 14

Safety and Handling

Important safety information for Apple TV

WARNING: To avoid injury, read the following safety information and the operating instructions before using Apple TV. Failure to follow these safety instructions could result in fire, electric shock, or other injury or damage to Apple TV or other property.

Important safety instructions

Read and follow these instructions to use Apple TV safely.

- Do not use Apple TV near water.

- Clean only with a dry cloth.

- Do not block any ventilation openings. Install in accordance with these instructions.

- Do not install near any heat sources such as radiators, heat registers, stoves, or other devices (including amplifiers) that produce heat.

- Protect the power cord from being walked on or pinched, particularly at the plugs and at the point where it exits from Apple TV.

- Only use attachments/accessories specified by Apple.

- Unplug Apple TV during lightning storms or when unused for   long periods of time.

- Refer all servicing to qualified service personnel. Servicing is   required when Apple TV has been damaged in any way, such as when the power cord or plug is   damaged, liquid has been spilled or objects have fallen into Apple TV, or Apple TV has been exposed   to rain or moisture, does not operate normally, or has been dropped.

Handling

Your Apple TV may be   damaged by improper storage or handling. Be careful not to drop Apple TV when transporting   it.

Repairing

Do not make   repairs yourself. If Apple TV is damaged or malfunctions, contact Apple or an Apple Authorized Service Provider. Repairs   by service providers other than Apple or an Apple Authorized Service Provider may not involve the use of Apple   genuine parts and may affect the safety and functionality of the device.

Battery

Don't attempt to replace the Siri Remote battery yourself—you may damage the battery, which could cause overheating, fire, and injury. The lithium-ion battery in the Siri Remote should be removed by Apple or an authorized service provider.

Power

Apple TV has no on/off switch. To disconnect Apple TV from power, unplug the power cord. Make sure the power cord is always easily accessible. When connecting or disconnecting Apple TV, always hold the plug by its sides. Keep fingers away from the metal part of the plug.

Location

Do not use Apple TV outdoors. Apple TV is an indoor product. Do not place naked flame sources, such as lighted candles, on or near Apple TV. Do not expose Apple TV to dripping or splashing, and do not place any object filled with liquid, such as a vase, on Apple TV. Do not move Apple TV if another device such as a TV, computer, or other electronic device is connected to it.

WARNING: To reduce the risk of fire or electric shock, do not expose Apple TV to rain, liquid, moisture, excessive heat, or naked flame.

Charging the Siri Remote

Charge the Siri Remote with the included Lightning cable, or with other third-party "Made for iPhone" Lightning cables, and a compatible power adapter that is compliant with USB 2.0 or later and with applicable country regulations and international and regional safety standards, including Audio, Video and Similar Electronic Apparatus – Safety Requirements (IEC 60065). Using counterfeit or damaged cables or chargers, or charging when moisture is present, can cause fire, electric shock, injury, or damage to the Siri Remote or other property. When you use a power adapter to charge the Siri Remote, make sure the Lightning cable is fully inserted into the power adapter before you plug the adapter into a power outlet. It's important to keep the Siri Remote and the power adapter in a well-ventilated area when in use or charging.

Lightning cable and connector

Avoid prolonged skin contact with the connector when the Lightning cable is plugged into a power source, because it may cause discomfort or injury. Avoid situations where your skin is in contact with the Lightning connector for a long period of time when it's plugged in. For example, while the Siri Remote is charging or while the Lightning cable is plugged into a power source, don't sit or sleep on it or place it under a blanket, pillow, or your body. Take special care if you have a physical condition that affects your ability to detect heat against the body.

Discoloration of the Lightning connector after regular use is normal. Dirt, debris, and exposure to liquids may cause discoloration. To remove the discoloration or if the cable becomes warm during use or won't charge the Siri Remote, disconnect the Lightning cable from your computer or power adapter and clean it with a soft, dry, lint-free cloth. Do not use liquids or cleaning products when cleaning the Lightning connector.

Medical device interference

The Apple TV and Siri Remote contain components and radios that emit electromagnetic fields. These electromagnetic fields may interfere with medical devices, such as pacemakers and defibrillators. Consult your physician and medical device manufacturer for information specific to your medical device and whether you need to maintain a safe distance of separation between your medical device and the Apple TV and Siri Remote. Stop using the Apple TV and Siri Remote if you suspect they are interfering with your medical device.

Medical conditions

If you have a medical condition that you believe could be affected by using Apple TV (for example, seizures, blackouts, eyestrain, or headaches), consult with your physician prior to using Apple TV.

Explosive and other atmospheric conditions

Using Apple TV and Siri Remote in any area with a potentially explosive atmosphere, such as areas where the air contains high levels of flammable chemicals, vapors, or particles (such as grain, dust, or metal powders), may be hazardous. Exposing Apple TV and Siri Remote to environments having high concentrations of industrial chemicals, including near evaporating liquified gasses such as helium, may damage or impair Apple TV and Siri Remote functionality. Obey all signs, and instructions.

Repetitive motion

When you perform repetitive activities such as playing games on Apple TV, you may experience occasional discomfort in your hands, arms, wrists, shoulders, neck, or other parts of your body. If you experience discomfort, stop those activities and consult a physician.

Important handling information for Apple TV
Cleaning and care

To clean Apple TV, unplug the power cord and all cables. Then use a soft, dry, lint-free cloth. Avoid getting moisture in openings. Don't use window cleaners, household cleaners, aerosol sprays, solvents, alcohol, ammonia, or abrasives to clean Apple TV.

WARNING: Do not attempt to open Apple TV or disassemble it. You run the risk of electric shock, and damage caused by disassembly is not covered by the limited warranty. No user-serviceable parts are inside.

Operating environment

Apple TV works best in ambient temperatures between 32° and 95° F (0° and 35° C) and can be stored at temperatures between -4° and 113° F (-20° and 45° C). While you're using Apple TV, it's normal for the case to get warm. The Apple TV case is designed to transfer heat from inside the unit to the cooler air outside.

Do not operate Apple TV in areas with significant amounts of airborne dust or particulate matter that might clog the ventilation openings.

Gaming

Hold the Siri Remote securely and avoid excessive motion when playing games on Apple TV. Use the Remote Loop (sold separately) and maintain a secure grip on the Siri Remote to prevent injury, or accidental damage to the Siri Remote or other property.

Device information

Information such as the model number, serial number, and electrical rating is located on the bottom of Apple TV. To find the serial number onscreen, in Settings , go to General > about.

Thank you for purchasing our user guide!

Made in the USA
Middletown, DE
01 March 2020

85619923R00144